50

YEARS OF MUSIC

THE SAINT PAUL
CHAMBER
ORCHESTRA

— DAVE KENNEY —

NODIN PRESS

Published by Nodin Press, LLC
530 N Third Street
Suite 120
Minneapolis, MN 55401
612-333-6300
www.nodinpress.com

Printed by Bolger Vision Beyond Print

Design by Joseph D.R. OLeary
www.VetoDesign.com

ISBN 978-193247279-0

50

YEARS OF MUSIC

THE SAINT PAUL
CHAMBER
ORCHESTRA

— DAVE KENNEY —

Contents

Foreword

———

There was a time, not so long ago, when it was customary to speak of the "Big Five" American orchestras. The ranking was an arbitrary one and is now so outdated that there is no need to reproduce it here. But all of the large ensembles in the United States (and today there are at least a dozen of them capable of making great music on any given night) can take some lessons from The Saint Paul Chamber Orchestra—in unity, creativity, integrity, civic responsibility, farsightedness, and sheer resilience.

From the beginning, the SPCO was different. In the "bigger is better" social environment of the late 1950s, the SPCO offered an early affirmation that small, too, could be beautiful. In a cultural milieu that too often elevates a grand Maestro above the rest of the musicians on the stage, a democratic spirit—and, eventually, a collective leadership—prevailed. The orchestra played not only in downtown Saint Paul but in distant suburbs, not only in concert halls but in schools, churches and synagogues. The SPCO has offered listeners a sonic world where works by Franz Joseph Haydn and John Cage might share a program, where Mozart and Messiaen were equally at home.

Here you will learn about Melvin Sipe Jr. from Fountain Inn, South Carolina, whose father sold some of the family chickens to buy his prodigious five-year-old son a miniature violin. Later, young Melvin, under the more euphonious name of Leopold Sipe, would provide initial artistic impetus for the fledgling SPCO. You will read about Dennis Russell Davies, the brilliant, shaggy young visionary who rode into Saint Paul on his motorcycle and turned the capital of Minnesota into a center of the musical avant-garde.

Here is Pinchas Zukerman, one of the finest violinists of his time (and perhaps an even better violist), who came to Saint Paul as music director and brought the orchestra new eminence—in concert halls across the country and around the globe, on the radio, and on an unprecedented number of commercial recordings.

Here is the legendary "triumvirate"—Christopher Hogwood, whose streamlined, energetic recordings of Baroque and Classical works had made him a superstar in the early music movement; Hugh Wolff, whom *The New York Times* had dubbed "the most promising young American conductor to come along in many years"; and the celebrated American composer John Adams—who joined forces to present a new model for artistic directorship in the late twentieth century.

And here are stories of the men and women who built the SPCO from the inside—of musicians who came to Saint Paul and ended up staying. *The Saint Paul Chamber Orchestra: 50 Years of Music* is also a story of deft, creative presidents and general managers. It is the story of board members who took it upon themselves to keep the music playing in troubled financial times.

Finally, this is the story of the everyday listeners who banded together to save the SPCO in the unprecedented "radiothon" of 1993 that raised almost three quarters of a million dollars in a single day. A total of 5,400 people from all over Minnesota pledged funds,

> And here are stories of the men and women who built the SPCO from the inside—of musicians who came to Saint Paul and ended up staying.

ranging from a grant of $50,000 to a 50-cent donation from a child who loved music.

Here are tales of glory—for example, of the SPCO's international debut in 1974, a week of performances in Western Europe, followed by stops in then-Communist Poland, Romania, Hungary, Czechoslovakia, and Yugoslavia. The tour remains the only occasion on which the United States Congress put its considerable muscle and funding behind a chamber orchestra.

The SPCO's travels in the United States had their fascinations, too. To keep costs low, the board deemed it more prudent to charter aircraft than to fly with a major line. However, the noisy, old DC-3s had a maximum capacity of twenty-eight passengers and, to accommodate its personnel (and meet regulations), the orchestra needed to recruit, for extra pay, what was then called a "stewardess" from its ranks. Cellist Daryl Skobba attended the requisite training and may have been the only designated chamber-orchestra flight attendant in history.

As far back as the tenure of Leopold Sipe, contemporary music was central to the SPCO mission, and twelve living composers were represented in the ten concerts offered in Sipe's last season. Since then, the SPCO has presented works by Samuel Barber, Aaron Copland, Virgil Thomson, Elliott Carter, Ernst Krenek, Gian-Carlo Menotti, Ellen Taaffe Zwilich, William Schuman, and dozens of others during their lifetimes. Special pride was always taken in creators who were long-time residents of the Twin Cities—Dominick Argento, Stephen Paulus, Libby Larsen, and others.

In an unusual twist, the SPCO adopted a radical artistic model, eliminating the position of music director and instead opening positions for several artistic partners, world-renowned conductors and musicians who each collaborate with the orchestra three weeks per season for a minimum of three seasons. The move permitted the musicians of the SPCO an unprecedented control over their own creative destinies.

As The Saint Paul Chamber Orchestra enters its second half century, it is time to pay tribute to those musicians and citizens who took a quirky, quixotic, perennially underfunded venture and turned it into an American treasure. Dave Kenney has a terrific story to tell, and the photographs and documents contained in this volume should provide some nostalgic pride for those who were there, as well as continuing inspiration for us all.

Tim Page
Pulitzer Prize-winning music critic
Los Angeles
September 2008

Introduction

———

The Saint Paul Chamber Orchestra's arrival at the ripe old age of fifty is indeed worthy of celebration. Unlike traditional symphony orchestras, chamber orchestras are a rare breed; longevity and stability are hardly characteristic descriptions. Chamber orchestra years are more akin to "dog years" than human years. Fifteen to twenty years is a really good run. The SPCO's fifty-year run is in many ways miraculous.

The Saint Paul Chamber Orchestra shares this rarefied air with only three other chamber orchestras, an international quartet of grand exemplars of the chamber orchestra, the other members of which are: Nicholas Harnoncourt's Vienna Concentus Musicus, founded in 1954, a distinguished group with seminal impact in establishing the historically informed performance practice of Music of the Baroque and Classical periods; Neville Mariner's Academy of St. Martin in the Field, founded in 1959, with the largest discography and touring history of any chamber orchestra in the world; and the London-based English Chamber Orchestra, founded in 1960, which has enjoyed a long, steady career.

The SPCO occupies a singular place in this select constellation of stars. It performs far more concerts annually than its other club members, it is the only one with a sustainable and large audience in its home town, and it is the only one whose audience provides its primary financial support. Tellingly, it is the only one whose repertoire now touches the music of five centuries! The SPCO lives as vigorously in the Music of the Baroque as it does in the Music of Our Time. The fact that the Twin Cities-based SPCO enjoys a competitive international career is all the more extraordinary, considering that its like-kind competition is based in major international musical centers.

In fairness, of course, any view of the SPCO's international standing must also take into account the chamber orchestras that do not meet the fifty-year test, for that span measures only longevity. There are other more complex factors, and here the SPCO story becomes more interesting. Many fine chamber orchestras enjoy but temporal impact, tied to the energies of individuals or groups of musicians around whose artistry they were founded.

In the latter category, Orpheus, the Chamber Orchestra of Europe, the Deutsche Kammerphilharmonie, and the Mahler Chamber Orchestra stand out as great chamber orchestras driven by the artistic desire and talents of their founding musicians. In the former, the Kremerata Baltica (Gidon Kremer), The Moscow Chamber Soloists (Vladimir Spivakov), and Il Giardino Harmonica (Giovanni Antonini) derive their ascendance from the artistic vision and energies of their individual founders.

There are still other examples of great chamber orchestras founded on a commitment to a specialty repertoire, particularly period instrument ensembles and contemporary music groups. Toronto's Tafelmusik, London's Orchestra of the Age of Enlightenment, the Freiburg Baroque Orchestra, and The Philharmonia Baroque, led by the SPCO's longtime collaborator Nicholas McGegan, are fine examples among many of period instrument ensembles. The London Sinfonietta, Frankfurt's Ensemble Modern, and New York's Bang on a Can All-Stars stand out in the new music area.

Collectively these eighteen chamber

orchestras (and arguably a few others) of exceedingly high quality make for a diverse, vibrant competitive international environment for the SPCO, which has evolved over its fifty-year history. And it is important to emphasize just how important these environmental changes have been in the SPCO's artistic development, exceeding even the powerful cultural changes we have seen in western society over the past fifty years. In the arcane world of international chamber orchestra competition, the SPCO has weathered not merely an explosion in the number of great chamber orchestras worldwide, but also a more fundamental change in the field away from "generalist" to "specialist" chamber orchestras.

It its own local environment it is also noteworthy that the SPCO and the Minnesota Orchestra "compete" in the only metropolitan area in America with two full-time, very high-quality professional orchestras, offering more concerts *per capita* each year than anywhere else in the country. Yes!— including New York, Chicago, Boston, San Francisco, and Los Angeles.

In short, the SPCO competes on quality of experience alone: with the easy maze of entertainment options available at home, each concert of the SPCO must be competitive as a superior artistic and social experience. Concerts must be powerful spiritual journeys, experienced collectively rather than in the isolation of one's living room.

Artistic profile has been the key, and has four simple but essential components: What, where, with whom and how we play. The "what" demands our commitment to music spanning five centuries, written for SPCO-sized ensembles. The "where" demands our presence not only in the world's great concert halls, but more importantly our affordable presence in churches, synagogues, community centers and concert halls throughout the Twin Cities. The "with whom" demands our consistent partnership with supremely gifted musical leaders and our unrelenting commitment to putting only the best players on stage in the SPCO. And the "how we play" trumps everything, for the SPCO must continually drive itself toward excellence in style and quality of performance. This is the *sine qua non* of survival, and the key to the SPCO's grand arrival at the august age of fifty.

Without faith in a compelling SPCO experience, why would thousands choose to venture out on cold winter nights, pay for parking and tickets and take several hours of their precious time to experience a concert collectively and live, when it would clearly be less expensive and more convenient to turn the radio on two days later to listen at home?

Building a distinct artistic profile over time has required sustained commitment to innovative thinking and a willingness to go against the grain of conventional thinking about how orchestras present themselves to their communities. Increasingly importantly, it has required the courage to alter traditional governance and decision-making practices, ranging from structure, strategic thinking, artistic planning, and extending to labor relations.

As early as the 1970s, the dynamic duo of Dennis Russell Davies as music director and Stephen Sell as managing director invented the "Music on the Move" concept, threw out white tie and tails for blue velvet suits and catapulted the SPCO to the forefront as a catalyst for new and experimental music. In the late 1980s, under the leadership of Deborah Borda, the SPCO's courage to replace the music director with the Artistic Commission of Hugh Wolff, Christopher Hogwood, and John Adams spoke to an imbedded willingness to try new and different approaches. During the 1990s, the SPCO's affiliations with Garrison Keillor, Bobby McFerrin, and Chick Corea were at the forefront of efforts to broaden public interaction with the orchestra.

During the past ten years, the SPCO has more clearly defined itself through the creation of an artistic leadership system in which SPCO musicians and management collaborate with each other and a group of internationally renowned artistic partners to provide a diversity of musical expression for the public previously unattainable under the old music director system. Similarly, the rapid expansion of the number of performance venues throughout the Twin Cities since 2005, combined with an aggressive reduction of ticket prices has resulted in a more than two-and-one-half-fold increase in subscriber households.

The engine behind these changes has been a fierce commitment to a collaboratively developed long-range vision for the SPCO. This has required, as noted, fundamental changes in how the SPCO does its business. The traditional lines of demarcation among board, orchestra, and staff have been intentionally blurred, yet retaining a clear understanding that each constituency plays distinct roles in the organization. The most compelling example resides in labor negotiations, wherein old-style confrontational tactics have receded in favor of efforts to reconcile contractual terms and conditions with long-range organizational and artistic goals—which include, significantly, the economic well-being and artistic development of SPCO musicians.

This conscious dismantling of age-old organizational silos has brought together a critical mass of musicians, volunteers, and staff far more motivated by ambition for long-term success of the whole organization than by the more narrow interests of their particular constituencies. This introduction is not the place for detailed discussion of these dynamics, but it is worth noting here that the power of far greater inclusiveness in decision-making has been a transformative force in the SPCO's ability to navigate its challenging environment nimbly enough to achieve its fiftieth year.

The centerpiece of the SPCO's fiftieth-anniversary celebration was the first-ever International Chamber Orchestras Festival held in several Twin Cities locations in January 2009. It is not by accident that the SPCO's guests were the Chamber Orchestra of Europe, The London Sinfonietta, The Orchestra of the Age of Enlightenment, and the Philharmonia Baroque. Indeed, it is a conscious effort to place the SPCO in its international context for audiences at home.

Thus, it is safe to argue that the SPCO stands alone in the world of chamber orchestras, unchallenged in the depth and breadth of its home town support, unmatched in the scope of its repertoire reach. Importantly, it is the only one in America whose musicians enjoy full-time employment.

That all of this has blossomed and flourished in the Twin Cities—not in London or Vienna—makes the SPCO's accomplishment all the more miraculous. And that is the quintessence of this book, which compellingly tells the story of the SPCO's roller-coaster ride ("non-linear progress" might be more polite!) from its modest and improbable beginnings, through its battles to define itself coherently to its community and itself, through its turbulent financial struggles, and, since its near-death experience in 1993, its maturation as an organization over the past fifteen years.

The 1993 crisis was a crucible for the SPCO. Thanks to the preceding thirty-five years of building of audience affection, the October 1993 weekend radiothon, ingeniously and generously aired by Minnesota Public Radio at the behest of Bill Kling, produced an extraordinary $700,000 in donations against a typically modest SPCO goal of $200,000. But the impact of the MPR radiothon was hardly limited to its financial support. MPR's generous intervention demonstrated to the community—and as importantly to the SPCO organization—that the SPCO *had* to survive, in stark contrast to nearly every other chamber orchestra in the world, which has sadly but proudly declared at some point "game over."

Thanks to the SPCO's courage to seize the opportunity offered up by the MPR radiothon, the story of the SPCO since 1993 demonstrates its incredible progress. On the strength of its MPR success, the SPCO was able to recruit its former general manager, Brent Assink, as SPCO president in 1994. Under his leadership, for the first time in its history, the SPCO made commitments to sustainable financial operations and to building a complete organization with a strong orchestra complemented by both a strong and stable staff and committed board of directors.

As we celebrate the miracle of the SPCO at fifty, there are several proud observations to share. First and foremost, the SPCO plays at home to a larger and more diverse audience than ever. Second, we celebrate the SPCO's undeniable standing as one of the world's great chamber orchestras. Third, we celebrate the SPCO's capacity to attract extremely talented and accomplished artists both to the ranks and the podium of the SPCO, chosen through exacting trials. Fourth, we celebrate the SPCO's ability to attract a powerful, generous and truly enlightened board of directors, which has in turn attracted scores of other generous and engaged volunteers in the governing members and friends and throughout the audience base. Fifth, we celebrate the fact that staff leadership openings have evolved into career destination positions. Financially, we celebrate the SPCO at fifty for having balanced its budget fourteen of the past fifteen years, with no accumulated deficit and not a penny of debt to anyone. Indeed, with an endowment size already in the top quartile of major American orchestras and a promising beginning to a new campaign, there is much to celebrate.

Looking forward through the haze of the current worldwide economic uncertainty, the SPCO's challenge will be its ability to serve its community compellingly by being woven into the very fabric of the metropolitan area, including, of course, in live performance. This idea is best articulated by Phillipe de Montebello, the retiring director of the Metropolitan Museum of Art, in the October 2008 *Atlantic*: "The public is a lot smarter than anybody gives it credit for. The public as a whole has intellectual curiosity. These are people who know the difference between a serious show and pure sham. If you take the high road, the public comes to expect it."

Nothing could be more true and more important to understand.

With appreciation and gratitude,

Bruce Coppock
SPCO President & Managing Director
1999-2008

Preface

———

It's a little after seven o'clock on the evening of the The Saint Paul Chamber Orchestra's penultimate 2007-2008 Ordway performance. I've planted myself on a stool backstage, off to the side. For a brief moment, I imagine that I'm an anthropologist out to document the behavior of a just-discovered indigenous tribe.

To my left stands the familiar wood-paneled arc that serves as the orchestra's performance background. From this vantage, it's nothing more than a two-story assemblage of scaffolding with a pair of doors leading onstage. Nearly everything—the backside of the set, the wiring and air ducts, the plastic tubs containing who knows what—is painted black. Four long tables arranged side-by-side stretch out in front of me.

Soon the musicians begin to arrive. One by one, they stake out places, draping jackets over the backs of chairs, placing instrument cases at corresponding spots on the four tables. I fumble through my program in an awkward attempt to figure out who's who.

Sabina Thatcher tunes her viola. Family photos line her open instrument case.

Bassoonist Charles Ullery walks by with two reeds protruding vampire-like from the corners of his mouth.

Flutist Alicia McQuerrey bursts a gum bubble.

Associate concertmaster Ruggero Allifranchini pops an Altoid mint and offers one to concertmaster Steven Copes. Copes accepts.

For a while, harpist Mollie Marcuson is the center of attention. She's arrived backstage sporting a new hair color: flaming orange.

"Did you do it yourself? I never have the guts to do it myself."

"Yikes! Egads!"

"There's something different about you. Glasses?"

"Introduce yourself to the new harp player, everyone."

"I like it."

Conductor Scott Yoo joins the growing throng of musicians about twenty minutes before the performance is scheduled to begin. Like everyone else, he's dressed in black, although he is the only one wearing a black t-shirt and black suspenders. Sipping water periodically from a small paper cup, he engages McQuerrey and Marcuson in a discussion of personal grooming habits.

It is somehow reassuring to discover that world-class musicians chew bubble gum, carry around family photos, and make jokes about each other's appearance, just as the rest of us do. It's easy to forget when you immerse yourself in an orchestra's history, as I have, that the making of music is, on its most basic level, a human endeavor, not an institutional one. Sit backstage in the minutes before a performance and it eventually will dawn on you that these musicians—these talented professionals who make such beautiful sounds night after night—are not much different from the people you typically encounter in the grocery store checkout line

With the clock nearing the top of the hour, technical manager Jon Kjarum begins pacing backstage, repeating his mantra: "Five minutes!" Most of the musicians have turned their attention to their instruments and are now creating a muted cacophony of dissonant sounds. As they play, they edge closer to the stage.

"Places, please."

Violinist Daria Adams slips on a pair of shiny black heels and joins her colleagues at the double doors leading onstage. A few stray notes from a double bass rumble in from somewhere nearby.

"Quiet, please."

It's 8:03 and the doors swing open. The musicians take their places onstage, basses bringing up the rear. Scott Yoo, seemingly oblivious to the orchestra's disappearance, wraps up a short conversation with keyboardist Skip James—something about a tricky entrance during the evening's second piece, Copland's *Clarinet Concerto*. Yoo tosses his paper cup into a wastebasket, takes a skipping start, and dashes out onstage to loud applause. After a brief silence, the sad, sustained opening tones of Jeffery Cotton's *Elegy* waft backstage.

As the evening progresses, I listen to various amalgamations of the orchestra play four strikingly different pieces. (The second half of the concert features Ives' *Three Places in New England* and Ginastera's *Variaciones concertantes*.) Through it all, the musicians display an informal backstage looseness that belies their onstage professionalism. Despite the stories I've heard about mercurial musicians, I see no evidence of egos run amok. After the Copland piece, Scott Yoo indicates to the evening's soloist, clarinetist Timothy Paradise, that they will return to the stage for a bow. But, just as they're about to head back out through the double doors, Yoo steps back, leaving Paradise to receive the audience's applause on his own. Yoo seems pleased with his deception.

My behind-the-scenes glimpse of the SPCO helps me gain a better understanding of the orchestra, but it goes only so far. No outsider can ever hope to fully comprehend and appreciate the complex human relationships that develop in the process of such high-level music making. I can't pretend to know whether these musicians always get along with each other as well as they seem to this night, but what I see and hear fits nicely with everything I've learned during the course of this project. Despite all the upheavals that the SPCO has experienced through the years—the financial crises, the venue hopping, the leadership changes—the musicians and the music they play have provided the continuity the orchestra needed to survive and thrive as an institution for half a century. To an observer perched on a backstage stool, it appears that this latest incarnation of the SPCO is more than capable of carrying on the tradition.

Dave Kenney

Chapter One
A Borrowed Band

It was a chilly Tuesday evening in late November 1963. The concert-going crowd included many of the Twin Cities' most reliably supportive arts patrons and a smattering of politicians—Governor Karl Rolvaag had sent his regrets— who generally only showed up for concerts when they were deemed big enough to be worth the bother. This occasion truly was something out of the ordinary. The evening's main attraction, The Saint Paul Chamber Orchestra, usually performed at its "home" auditorium in Saint Paul's Central High School. Even when it ventured away from Central High, it never crossed the Mississippi River into the realm of its much bigger and older competitor, the Minneapolis Symphony Orchestra. On this night, however, the twenty-seven-piece ensemble from Saint Paul was out to show that it

Keyboardist Layton "Skip" James, who joined The Saint Paul Chamber Orchestra in 1969, is one of only two current SPCO musicians to play under the direction of Leopold Sipe. Oboist Tom Tempel is the other.

Left: Leopold Sipe directs The Saint Paul Chamber Orchestra in a performance at the Saint Paul City Hall and Ramsey County Courthouse, November 13, 1970.

was more than a provincial upstart. It was making its Minneapolis debut in one of the nation's newest and most celebrated performance spaces—the Guthrie Theater.

In many respects, the Guthrie was a strange choice for such a debut. Its acoustics—meticulously crafted for the spoken word—lacked the reverberation that brought music to life. Its thrust stage, which jutted out into the auditorium, forced the orchestra to rearrange itself on a confined platform nearly surrounded by audience members.

Conductor Leopold Sipe entered the theater to enthusiastic applause and ascended the podium. Before him were three rows of players—brass and timpani farthest back, then woodwinds, then strings. Sipe was a commanding presence—tall, almost lanky, with silvering temples and an on-stage formality that matched his white tie and tails. He raised his baton, fixed his gaze on the back row, and cued the ensemble. A timpani roll and trumpet fanfare announced the orchestra's arrival in Minneapolis. From there, the evening followed a pattern typical of Sipe's programming: a healthy dose of Baroque (Purcell and Vivaldi); a lesser-known Mozart concerto; a post-intermission dive into the twentieth century (William Schuman); and a Haydn finale.

The audience was enchanted. The critics raved. The *Minneapolis Star*'s Edwin Bolton was especially taken with the ensemble's rendition of Schuman's Symphony No. 5 ("*Symphony for Strings*").

> *It was remarkably well realized, in the tense, straining first movement that arrived at hints of a breakthrough; in the showdown of the very slow middle section, introduced by a hauntingly beautiful violin solo line (played by Henry Kramer), and in an uninhibited finish that had bright tunes skipping happily all over the orchestra.*

St. Paul Pioneer Press critic John Harvey praised the orchestra for playing its "crispest and most elaborate best." It was a pity, he wrote, that the SPCO could not play "all its concerts in the Tyrone Guthrie theater."

The Saint Paul Chamber Orchestra, under the direction of Leopold Sipe, rehearses for its Minneapolis debut at the new Guthrie Theater.

Sipe and his players appreciated the positive reviews, but they couldn't shake the feeling that the audience and the critics were too forgiving. "There were many 'Oohs' and 'Aahs' and comments after the concert," Sipe recalled many years later, "[but] the sound [in the Guthrie] was bad for music, dry as an old dog's bone ... We gave it two seasons then quit before anyone caught on to the hoax."

The Saint Paul Chamber Orchestra was only in its fifth season by the time it made its Minneapolis debut in 1963. Hardly anyone remembered that the efforts leading to its creation had started fourteen years earlier.

Beginnings

In the fall of 1949, the leaders of some of Saint Paul's most active cultural organizations decided it was time to confront what they considered a looming cultural crisis. The city had always had its share of cultural institutions. The Minnesota Historical Society, the Minnesota Museum of Art, and the Schubert Club (a sponsor of recitals by renowned musicians) all dated back to the previous century. A few orchestral groups, including the Saint Paul Symphony Orchestra (founded in 1907) and the original Saint Paul Chamber Orchestra (approximately 1931 to 1933), had come and gone over the years. Longer-lived organizations such as the Science Museum of Minnesota (founded in 1907) and the Saint Paul Opera (founded in 1933) had further strengthened the city's cultural reputation. But now, on the eve of a new postwar decade, Saint Paul's long-held devotion to the arts seemed to be waning, its aspirations to cultural greatness relegated to the past. Sensing that something was wrong, these concerned leaders set out to determine the state of the city's cultural health; they convinced the Saint Paul Junior League to sponsor a survey. The results, while not surprising, proved catalytic.

The survey, conducted by a New York research firm, found that Saint Paul, more than most other cities of similar size, had failed over the years to reap "substantial benefit from the cultural generosity of one or more of its early leading families." As a result, the authors concluded, the city lacked a "physical rallying point"—a large endowed museum or an opera house—capable of nurturing the community's interest in the arts and sciences. Most of the old theaters that had once enlivened downtown, including the soon-to-be-demolished Garrick Theater (the former Grand Opera House) on West Sixth Street, had disappeared. The Civic Auditorium, with a seating capacity of more than three thousand, was too big for many musical, theatrical, and dance productions. The study's main conclusion: Saint Paul needed a community arts center.

With the results of the survey in hand, the cultural groups that participated in the study banded together to advocate for a new shared arts space. Although their ultimate goal, the construction of a new arts center, would go unrealized for another decade, their efforts spawned a new organization that would have a profound impact on the city's cultural life. The Saint Paul Council of Arts and Sciences (the Arts Council), founded in March 1954, initially focused almost exclusively on the drive to build a new arts center, but after a few years, it expanded its vision well beyond bricks and mortar.

No one was more crucial to the growth and success of the Arts Council than Ralph Burgard, the man who became its executive director in 1957. Burgard was a former advertising executive who had switched careers after a mid-life health scare. Before coming to Saint Paul, he had managed orchestras in Buffalo, New York, and Providence, Rhode Island, and had served as executive secretary of one of the nation's first local arts councils in Winston-Salem, North Carolina. Burgard was among the most passionate advocates of the arts council movement that took root in communities throughout the nation during the 1950s. He believed that communities could reinvigorate themselves by mobilizing popular support for the arts, and he was convinced Saint Paul was ready for such a mobilization.

By the late 1950s, Saint Paul, like many other urban areas, was in decline. Postwar prosperity, the baby boom, and a new reliance on automobiles (and highways) were combining to draw people and businesses out of the city and into the suburbs. Between 1948 and 1954, Saint Paul's downtown shopping district suffered a 15 percent decline in retail sales. Major employers such as 3M (Maplewood) and Univac (Eagan) were relocating. "Any vision of a great tradition in Saint Paul was pretty much down at the ears," Burgard said. "The downtown was fading."

Compounding the problems caused by suburban competition was what Burgard called Saint Paul's "inferiority complex" with regards to Minneapolis. Saint Paul had once been known as "the cultured city," he said. Now, as the exodus to the suburbs sucked life from the urban core, the older of the two cities had lost its cultural edge. Burgard was finding it difficult to convince anyone outside of the Arts Council to "take up the gauntlet of cultural advocacy."

About a year after arriving in Saint Paul, Burgard orchestrated the formation of a new organization, under the umbrella of the Arts Council, that would focus on the one artistic discipline he considered most ripe for revival: music. The Saint Paul Philharmonic Society, incorporated in the fall of 1958, was a gathering of well-connected

Officers of the newly created St. Paul Philharmonic Society look over the organization's articles of incorporation, November 1, 1958. Left to right: Vice President Hamilton S. Ross, Secretary Jean West, President Lawrence Platt, Jr., and Treasurer Louis M. Klass.

Saint Paulites whose musical expertise was limited at best. "We were not musicians," the Philharmonic's first president, Larry Platt, recalled years later. "We were simply lay people who were interested in music."

The Philharmonic's goals reflected Burgard's belief that the success of any arts program depended on community support. Its plan included three initiatives designed specifically to encourage the community's involvement with music: a new youth orchestra, a music-in-the-schools program, and an amateur community orchestra. There was one other element of the plan that Burgard considered the "crown jewel": At his urging, the Philharmonic Society stated its intention to create a professional chamber orchestra.

The city already had one orchestra—the Saint Paul Civic Orchestra—which had debuted in 1949. The Civic, as it was widely known, was a large ensemble of sixty to seventy players, many of them amateurs. It had no paid conductor and it attracted miniscule audiences, but its members and supporters considered it a valuable community asset. It was, in the words of one board member, "a workshop type of activity" that trained young musicians and gave amateurs a chance to play.

Looming even larger than the Civic over Saint Paul's cultural landscape was the professional orchestra on the other side of the Mississippi River. The Minneapolis Symphony Orchestra was a ninety-plus-piece ensemble nearing its fiftieth anniversary. Although some believed it had taken a step back in quality when conductor Antal Dorati replaced the dynamic Dmitri Mitropoulos in 1949, it still ranked among the finest orchestras in the country.

Burgard was well aware that the Minneapolis Symphony and the Saint Paul Civic Orchestra both enjoyed strong support in the community, but he remained convinced the city of Saint Paul needed more music—better music—if it were to achieve its cultural potential. It needed its own professional orchestra, one that aspired to musical excellence (unlike the Civic) and that complemented, rather than competed with, the Minneapolis Symphony.

Burgard believed a chamber orchestra was the perfect cure for Saint Paul's musical malaise. A chamber orchestra with between twenty and thirty players would provide a clear alternative to the Minneapolis Symphony. It would be much smaller and would have the versatility to play a wide range of musical works, from Baroque to contemporary, that larger orchestras tended to ignore. It would offer a higher level of musicianship than the Saint Paul Civic Orchestra had ever provided. Chamber orchestras, with a smaller complement of players, had little room for mediocrity. "We had to have something that had real quality ... in which Saint Paul could take real pride," Burgard said.

In his dual role as executive director of the Arts Council and behind-the-scenes visionary of the Philharmonic, Burgard began carefully nurturing his chamber orchestra plans. Under his leadership, the Arts Council launched a campaign in early 1959 to raise $150,000 for the council's member organizations—including the yet-to-be-formed chamber orchestra. Then he turned his attention to the biggest obstacle standing in his way: the Civic.

Many members of the Saint Paul Civic Orchestra assumed that they would form the nucleus of Burgard's new chamber orchestra. Burgard did not intend to let that happen.

> *I felt that the chamber orchestra should be the best musicians we could capture in the Twin Cities—that they should not just be Civic Orchestra musicians. Right from the beginning we avoided that because the Civic Orchestra didn't have very good musicians. They had some, but most of them were not of the caliber we needed for a chamber orchestra.*

At the same time, Burgard knew that he could not afford to antagonize the Civic and its supporters. Many of the Civic's players were members of the local musicians' union, and the union wielded considerable power and influence. Among other things, it controlled a pot of trust fund money, distributed by the American Federation of Musicians, which was meant to pay for the presentation of free public concerts by union musicians.

Determined to keep the Civic separate from his chamber orchestra and intrigued by the prospect of tapping the union trust fund money, Burgard engineered a merger. In January 1959, the Saint Paul Civic Orchestra's union directors combined with the board of the Saint Paul Philharmonic Society to form a new community music organization, the Saint Paul Civic Philharmonic Society. (The society would eventually drop the word "Civic" from its name.) Under the merger agreement, the Civic Orchestra would add musicians and lengthen its season, but would remain a community ensemble distinct from the still-to-be-created chamber orchestra. The trust fund money would conveniently go into a joint account. "The Civic Orchestra people were always suspicious of me, and rightly so," Burgard said. "They suspected I was doing an end run. And I was."

Tensions with the union reached their climax a few months after the merger when Burgard engaged Sam Flor, an assistant personnel manager with the Minneapolis Symphony, to begin recruiting players for the chamber orchestra. With his contacts on the other side of the river, Flor quickly revealed a preference for Minneapolis musicians. Members of the Civic, many of whom still harbored hopes of playing with the chamber orchestra, felt slighted.

Burgard, who had encouraged Flor's hiring of Minneapolis musicians, suddenly faced what he called a "growing rebellion." At two consecutive board meetings in the summer of 1959, the union faction of the Philharmonic's board tried to fire Flor and replace him with a union contractor, who presumably would be more willing to hire Civic Orchestra musicians. When it appeared at the second meeting that the union directors would finally succeed, Philharmonic President Larry Platt—who had previously abstained from voting—cast the deciding vote in favor of retaining Flor. The union faction was incensed, but Ralph Burgard was elated. The line between the Civic and the chamber orchestra had been maintained. "That vote really saved the chamber orchestra," he recalled years later. "Without that crucial benchmark ... the old Civic Orchestra would have run it into the ground."

Building an Orchestra

Even as Sam Flor recruited musicians, a search committee appointed by the Philharmonic board was actively looking for a music director to lead the chamber orchestra and oversee the Philharmonic's other programs. The job description was demanding. The music director had to be a conductor of "outstanding and proven ability," a maestro capable of mingling with audiences, instructing young musicians, and charming potential donors. The chosen candidate also had to be willing to accept a salary of $8,000 a year.

In the weeks following the job posting, the search committee received about six dozen applications from around the country and overseas. Most of the applicants were willing to accept a paltry salary for the opportunity to create what promised to be one of the world's few permanent and regularly performing chamber orchestras. Many were only marginally qualified, but one was especially intriguing. World-renowned violinist Roman Totenberg (the father of future National Public Radio legal affairs correspondent

Leopold and Elaine Sipe look on as their daughter, five-year-old Suzanne, draws a bow across the $3.95 violin on which her father learned to play.

Nina Totenberg) had long dreamed of starting a chamber orchestra and he seemed genuinely interested in the job. The search committee brought him to Saint Paul for an interview. It even invited him to sample the acoustics at the Central High School auditorium, where the orchestra would present most of its concerts. Totenberg was willing to go only so far in pursuit of the position. He did not want to move to Saint Paul—at least not permanently. He proposed an arrangement by which he would conduct ten to twelve weeks each season while continuing to perform around the world. The search committee, while tempted, rejected his proposal. "We weren't ready for that," Burgard explained. "[We needed] a full-time music director who made his roots here ... [not] a professional musician who came flitting in from New York and back there again."

Then an unlikely candidate appeared.

Leopold Sipe had nothing approaching the professional pedigree of Roman Totenberg. A native of both North and South Carolina, he was a thirty-five-year-old violinist with only a few years' professional conducting experience at the Charlotte Opera and the Tacoma Symphony Orchestra in Washington. But he came highly recommended by world-famous conductor Willem Van Otterloo, who ran the International Conductors Seminar in the Netherlands. (Sipe had recently completed Otterloo's three-week course and had prevailed on the esteemed conductor to send a telegram extolling his suitability for the Saint Paul job: "SIPE FIRST CLASS. TAKE HIM.") When his application failed to generate a response, Sipe called Ralph

Burgard and offered to drive to Minnesota for an interview. Although Burgard's tone over the phone seemed to Sipe lukewarm at best, the administrator in Saint Paul said he would be glad to meet with the young conductor if he wanted to make the trip.

The job applicant who showed up at Burgard's door in the summer of 1959 was a handsome beanpole of a man with a thick drawl and quick smile. It didn't take long for his innate charm to work its magic. Sipe described to Burgard his vision of "the future of the orchestra" and expressed his willingness to build community support for the all Philharmonic's music programs, not just the chamber orchestra. Burgard was impressed. When the interview was complete, he took the young Carolinian to the homes of several board members so they could meet the man who was about to become the first music director of The Saint Paul Chamber Orchestra.

Sipe moved to Saint Paul in September 1959 and immediately set to work on assembling his orchestra. Following Sam Flor's example, he plucked almost all his players from the ranks of the Minneapolis Symphony. (Only two musicians from the Saint Paul Civic Orchestra, violinist Ted Ptashne and flutist Mary Wilson, made the cut.) At the same time, he embraced the community relations aspect of his job—meeting and greeting potential donors in the living rooms of some of the city's most prominent families, granting interviews to reporters, and talking up the virtues of the Philharmonic Society's programs at gardening clubs, fraternal organizations, and houses of worship. It wasn't long before Leopold Sipe became a social fixture in Saint Paul. "He did everything we could expect of him," Burgard said.

Two months after Sipe's arrival in Minnesota, on the evening of Wednesday, November 18, 1959, the thirty-one-piece Saint Paul Chamber Orchestra debuted at the Central High School auditorium. The audience was tiny, only about 150 people, but those who attended enjoyed an eclectic program that would serve as a template for what was to come. As the program notes explained, the SPCO planned to devote itself to "the wonderful literature, both classic and contemporary, that is not ordinarily played by large symphonies." The debut concert opened with Sipe's arrangement of Purcell's *Ceremonial Music* and then, as promised, alternated between the "classic"—Bach's *Brandenberg Concerto No. 1* and Mozart's Symphony No. 35 ("Haffner")—and the "contemporary" —Wayne Barlow's *The Winter's Passed* and Ernest Bloch's Concerto Grosso No. 2.

Saint Paul Pioneer Press music critic John Harvey, who would soon establish himself as one of the orchestra's most ardent supporters, hailed the event as "something new, something different, and what is more important, something very good."

Sipe projected a formal, almost austere, presence on stage.

The young conductor is a sound choice for the job. He knows his music and he knows his craft. He seems to have absorbed from Pierre Monteux, with whom he studied, the ability to get the maximum results with a minimum of fuss and feathers. He has feeling and temperament, too, and a fine knowledge of style...

It is both exciting and deeply satisfying to hear Mozart's symphony done with the proper balance between strings and winds. There is an entirely different sound, lighter, gayer and more open than when played by a regulation symphony orchestra.

The November 18 performance was the first of four concerts that the SPCO presented during its debut season. Although the critics in both Saint Paul and Minneapolis were kind (*Minneapolis Star* reviewer John Sherman, for example, praised the orchestra for its "enterprising spirit" and its refusal to adopt a "just-another-concert" approach), the slapdash nature of the enterprise was hard to miss. Sipe was shouldering almost every burden associated with the concerts—from typing programs to setting up chairs in the auditorium—and sometimes the strain showed. On the evening of the second concert in early December, Sipe was horrified to discover that the chairs and music stands he had carefully arranged on the auditorium's stage were gone, replaced by set pieces for a student play. Sipe and his wife, Elaine, dragged furniture off the stage themselves and returned the players' chairs and stands to their proper places. It didn't help that Sipe was scheduled that night to make his Saint Paul debut as an instrumentalist in Bach's Concerto for Two Violins. "I was plenty tired from pulling all that furniture around," he later recalled.

Money was a constant worry. The orchestra was depending on Burgard's Arts Council to provide most of its funding, but the council was having trouble meeting its $150,000 fundraising goal. With ticket sales languishing and the Arts Council contribution on hold, the SPCO had no cash flow to speak of. "We were not earning enough money from ticket sales," recalled Hamilton Ross, Larry Platt's successor as council president. "I remember at intermission standing up and counting heads ... to see how much money we made, hoping we'd have enough money to write a check."

When there wasn't enough cash to pay the musicians, treasurer Louis Klaus opened his wallet to make sure their checks didn't bounce. When the Philharmonic's end-of-the-year books showed a $2,000 deficit, its board members quietly made additional donations to make up the difference. It wasn't until January 1960—when the Arts Council completed its fund drive and wrote a check to cover Sipe's salary—that the orchestra's fiscal worries finally subsided. Only Sipe seemed unconcerned about the orchestra's money problems. "Any deficit is unfortunate," he wrote in a letter to the board, "but it is my opinion that this particular deficit is actually an *investment* for the future, rather than a deficit of the past."

In his review of the SPCO's first season, critic John Harvey was less willing than Sipe to gloss over the orchestra's fiscal troubles. "Sipe showed excellent musical practicality and a shrewd sense of values in budgeting the rehearsal time available," he wrote. "Still, the first season underscored the necessity for obtaining more funds to provide the working time the orchestra needs to realize its full potential."

Beyond the Chamber Orchestra

Once Sipe completed his first season with the SPCO, he turned his attention to the other three programs the Philharmonic Society had hired him to oversee: a proposed music-in-the-classroom initiative (for fourth-, fifth-, and sixth-graders); a yet-to-be-formed youth orchestra (for junior and senior high school students); and a reconstituted Saint Paul Civic Orchestra (for adult amateurs). Although the classroom program soon fell by the wayside, the other two blossomed under Sipe's leadership.

The youth orchestra, while ultimately successful, was slow to develop. When Sipe put out a call for young musicians in early 1960, only about fifteen showed up for the first meeting, and none played a string instrument. Unwilling to oversee an ensemble consisting exclusively of flutes, trumpets, and saxophones, Sipe temporarily abandoned his youth orchestra plans. When he sent out a promotional flyer the following fall, he included an offer to arrange rentals for any youngster who wished to play the violin, viola, or cello. (Chamber Orchestra violinist Ted Ptashne, who owned a music shop, was happy to supply the instruments.) The offer worked. Sipe quickly assembled a well-balanced orchestra of thirty-five eager elementary school students. Over the next three years, the Philharmonic Society's youth program expanded to include five ensembles made up of 121 students of various ages and talents.

The youth orchestra also spawned an offshoot that was arguably the most popular and successful of the Philharmonic's early programs. In the summer of 1962, Sipe and Elaine Springsted, the mother of one of the youth orchestra's musicians, started a summer music camp. The first, just one week long, was a makeshift affair held at a Boy Scout camp in Bass Lake, Minnesota. Response from the twenty-five students was so enthusiastic that Sipe and Springsted felt compelled to expand the program. The next year, the young musicians took up residence at a larger Boy Scout camp on the Saint Croix River. A second session was added. Enrollment jumped to eighty students. The following year, more than 150 students attended. The camp remained popular throughout the 1960s and attracted several young musicians who went on to forge impressive careers, including guitarist Sharon Isbin and future SPCO violinist Elsa Nilsson. The students played in

The Philharmonic Society's summer music camp **(above)** and its music-in-the-classroom program **(below)** both relied on SPCO musicians to provide hands-on instruction. Shown here: Edouard Blitz helps a cello student with his bowing technique as violist Salvatore Venittelli looks on, 1969.

ensembles, studied music theory, and received private instruction from members of The Saint Paul Chamber Orchestra. One of the instructors, cellist Eddie Blitz, was amazed at how the kids responded to Sipe's demanding schedule.

> *The camp day would be lessons in the morning, then chamber music for another hour. Theory classes in the afternoon. More playing in the afternoon, and then at night if you wanted to play, you played. I mean it was around the clock. I don't know how these kids took it, but they went bananas over it. And we were turned on because of the enthusiasm.*

Sipe also had responsibility for developing the Civic Orchestra. In its original incarnation, the Civic was a hybrid group of amateur and professional, unionized musicians. The merger of the Civic and the Philharmonic Society had begun a process of separating the amateurs from the professionals. By the time Sipe arrived in Minnesota, the lines were clear: The new SPCO was Saint Paul's professional orchestra; the Civic was for amateurs. During its first season under Sipe's direction, the Civic had only twenty members and performed just two concerts. Sipe worked diligently to build the orchestra and improve its sound. By 1964, the Civic had grown to fifty players and was putting on five free concerts a year.

Under Sipe's leadership, the youth orchestra, the summer camp, and the reinvigorated Civic Orchestra helped build community support for the Philharmonic Society and its crown jewel, the SPCO. Sipe handled his multiple responsibilities with aplomb and rarely complained about the heavy workload. He agreed with Burgard that the chamber orchestra's survival depended largely on his ability to build a corps of music lovers in Saint Paul. Still, that didn't mean he enjoyed working with children or amateur musicians. "Leopold hated conducting [the Civic] and hated conducting the youth orchestra," Burgard later recalled. "He was willing to only because we felt we had to have this community base." The chamber orchestra was Sipe's true professional passion, and he had big plans for its future.

Aiming Higher

The SPCO's 1963-1964 season was a breakthrough of sorts. Not only did the orchestra make its Minneapolis debut at the Guthrie Theater, it produced its first recording. Side one of the LP disc, recorded at Saint Paul's Prom Ballroom, included two pieces by local composers: Gene Gutche's *Bongo Divertimento*, and Paul Fetler's *Nothing But Nature*. Side two featured just one piece: Haydn's Symphony No. 73. Without a contract from an established record label, Sipe, with investments from several members of the orchestra and the Philharmonic board, formed the Saint Paul Recording Company to release and distribute the album. Although hopes were high that the LP would bring national exposure, the lack of support from a national record label proved crippling. In

Without a true concert hall to call its own, the SPCO played in a variety of acoustically suspect venues during its first decade.

a letter to his musicians, Sipe suggested they try to drum up sales as they toured with the Minneapolis Symphony. "Stop in the record shops in cities and towns where you are playing," he wrote. "You need not identify yourself. Just indicate your interest in the orchestra and album."

After four years of nurturing all of the Philharmonic Society's programs, Sipe was itching to concentrate exclusively on the SPCO and to expand the orchestra's reputation beyond Saint Paul. With the conclusion of the 1963-1964 season, he and the Philharmonic Society board began laying out plans for the future. A 1964 planning document committed the society to establishing "a full-time resident chamber orchestra" that presented extended concert series in the Twin Cities and toured both nationally and abroad. A similar document drawn up the following year asserted time was of the essence. "There is no longer any doubt that the transition from musicians hired on a 'job-contract' basis to ones engaged for specific services on a full time basis must be made with careful haste," it read. "Existing conditions are no longer tenable if growth and maximum quality are to be maintained."

Sipe had been lobbying for at least a year to turn what he called his "borrowed" orchestra into a full-time resident ensemble, but his arguments took on new urgency during the fall of 1965. The Minneapolis Symphony had recently approved a new contract guaranteeing its musicians forty-five weeks of steady employment by 1970. That meant the musicians currently playing for the SPCO—almost all of whom also played for the Minneapolis Symphony—would soon be too busy to perform in Saint Paul. Seeking to turn this seemingly bad news to his advantage, Sipe went to his biggest booster in the Twin Cities press corps, *Saint Paul Pioneer Press* critic John Harvey. He clued Harvey in to the challenge posed by the Minneapolis Symphony's new contract and then waited to see what showed up in the newspaper. Harvey did not disappoint.

> *In these fast-moving times no organization can stand still. The St. Paul Chamber orchestra, as a cultural organization unique in this area, owes it to itself, the community it serves and the city whose name it bears to grow and flourish. This means, eventually, more concerts, touring activities and more rehearsals.*
>
> *But can this be done under conditions of dependence on Minneapolis Symphony personnel, who may become less and less available? Will this not require, sooner than we think, hiring top-grade professionals not employed by the Minneapolis orchestra—which will entail reasonably full employment at good salaries, and which in turn will involve a much larger financial outlay? Will events, in short, force the St. Paul Chamber Orchestra to go major-league to continue?*

In the days following the publication of Harvey's article, Sipe stepped up his lobbying effort—turning for support to some of the Twin Cities' most influential citizens. Governor Karl Rolvaag, Saint Paul Mayor George Vavoulis, and Minneapolis Mayor Art Naftalin wrote letters to Philharmonic President Louis Lundgren, urging him and the society's board of directors to approve Sipe's expansion plans. Arts Council President C. E. Bayliss Griggs chimed in, assuring Lundgren that "we stand ready to assist you" should the Philharmonic decide to turn the SPCO into a full-time orchestra. (Griggs did not indicate, however, whether the Arts Council's assistance would include more money.)

A few months later, on February 25, 1966, the Philharmonic Society Board of Directors gave Sipe part of what he wanted. It voted to establish a "core resident orchestra"—essentially a small ensemble within the orchestra, made up of full-time, professional musicians unaffiliated with the Minneapolis Symphony. In addition to their regular duties with the SPCO, these musicians would be expected to perform in smaller chamber groups, teach classes at local colleges, and provide instruction at the society's summer camp. The assumption was that if everything went well, the society would gradually add more core musicians until the entire SPCO consisted of full-time professionals. Although Sipe had hoped to add at least a few full-time players in time for the upcoming 1966-1967 season, the Philharmonic board decided to delay implementation of the plan until the following year.

Sipe's dreams were finally coming true. His orchestra had recorded its first album and the Philharmonic Society's board had approved, in principle, his plan to transform the SPCO into a full-time, resident orchestra.

Now all he needed was to make a big splash on the national stage.

In May 1966, Sipe and the SPCO embarked on their first performing tour outside Minnesota. The first stop was Manhattan, Kansas; the last stop was Manhattan, New York. For a group that had gone years with little national recognition, this engagement in New York was exhilarating. Billed as a concert party, the orchestra's appearance in the ballroom of the Biltmore Hotel may have lacked the cachet of a concert at Carnegie Hall or the then-new Lincoln Center, but it still qualified as a New York debut. It hardly mattered that the music was accompanied by silverware clinking against china—it was New York. In its generally positive review of the performance, the *New York Times* described the orchestra as a "good, earnest group." Back home, critic John Harvey put the event in perspective, explaining that the SPCO's New York debut was just part of a plan to create an orchestra that "would redound to the credit of St. Paul in the eyes of the nation."

That plan took another big step toward fruition a year later, when the Philharmonic Society announced a series of significant changes for the SPCO's upcoming 1967-1968 season. The orchestra was moving into a new home, the recently redesigned and expanded Crawford Livingston Theater in the Saint Paul Arts and Science Center. (The Arts Council had opened the center three years earlier, but its theater was too small to accommodate most SPCO concerts.) It had hired a new business manager, George Michaelson, to raise money and take over many of the administrative tasks Sipe had previously handled. Most significant, it was opening the season with nine new full-time resident musicians: violinists Henry Gregorian and Judith Yanchus; violist Salvatore Venittelli; cellist Cynthia Eddy Britt; flutist Mary Roberts Wilson; oboist Ian Wilson; clarinetist Michael Sutyak; bassoonist Maxine Elworthy; and French hornist Marvin McCoy.

Sipe was elated that his "borrowed" orchestra was finally beginning to look like the resident ensemble he had always dreamed of conducting. "The big advantage," he said, "is that [these players] are not going to be fluctuating back and forth from the large orchestra [the Minneapolis Symphony] to the small orchestra as they have had to do in the past." Switching between the two groups was difficult, he explained, because each orchestra relied on very different concepts of playing. "Playing in a chamber orchestra is like being out there on a stage in your bathing suit," he said. "It's very exciting. You're constantly exposed and you can't goof off for a minute."

The nine musicians of the new orchestra core formed two small groups—a string quartet and a woodwind quintet—that performed in towns throughout the Upper Midwest. They also served as music instructors at the College of Saint Catherine and

Leopold Sipe during the recording of the SPCO's first album—an LP disc featuring the works of Gene Gutche, Paul Fetler, and Joseph Haydn, 1964.

Hamline University. Within the orchestra, their moonlighting activities earned them the nickname, "Leopold's Leftovers."

Sipe and the orchestra's new business manager, George Michaelson, believed the touring successes of the string quartet and the woodwind quintet provided a template for the larger SPCO and other similarly sized orchestras. "We are, in effect, writing the book for towns of this size around the country on how to [tour]," Michaelson said. Now it was a matter of filling out the orchestra's ranks with resident musicians who had time to travel.

On September 15, 1968, the opening night of the 1968-1969 season, a small audience braved severe weather to attend the debut concert of what Michaelson dubbed "the new Saint Paul Chamber Orchestra." For the first time in its history, the SPCO could claim that all of its musicians—all twenty-one of them—were full-time employees who did not have to split their allegiance with another orchestra. Five of the core musicians who had been hired the previous year—Gregorian, Yanchus, Venittelli, Wilson, and Britt—were back. So were five former part-timers: violist Myrna Janzen, bassoonist Max Metzger, hornist Leslie Blake, oboist Lynn Shafer, and bassist Susan Matthew. (Shafer and Matthew were both alumni of the Philharmonic's youth program.) The other eleven musicians came from all parts of the country and were new to the SPCO.

The revamped SPCO got off to something of an inauspicious start (John Harvey, whose reviews were almost always glowing, noted in his critique of the debut concert that "some flaws in ensemble were apparent"), but there was no denying the orchestra had reached a milestone. The SPCO was now one of only two full-time, professional, and community-funded chamber ensembles in the country, and the other one—the Chamber Symphony of Philadelphia—was on the verge of bankruptcy. Sipe, who had been waiting years for this moment, was delighted to hand his duties with

With the addition of full-time resident musicians during the late 1960s, the SPCO began splitting itself into small traveling ensembles. **Above:** Daryl Skobba, Hanley Daws, John Gaska, and Carolyn Daws of the "Daws Quartet," 1970. **Below:** Baroque Ensemble members Susan Matthew (bass), John Howell (violin), Thomas Tempel (oboe), James Preston (bassoon), Yuko Heberlein (violin), Layton "Skip" James (harpsichord), Lawrence Barnhart (horn), Mark Zimmerman (violin), and Bruce Allard (violin), 1971.

the Civic Orchestra and the Philharmonic Society's youth programs to one of his new hires, violinist Ralph Winkler. Everything seemed to be going according to plan—except the touring.

For months George Michaelson had been assuring Sipe and the Philharmonic board that he was close to nailing down two extensive tours for the 1968-1969 season: a fall tour of Minnesota, North Dakota, and Canada; and a February tour of eight cities east of the Mississippi including New York. As the new season got underway, it became clear that Michaelson had promised more than he could deliver. Both tours fell through. The news was a major disappointment for Sipe and his musicians, who had been looking forward to hitting the road. Michaelson resigned under a cloud, but not before lucking into another tour that softened the blow of his earlier scheduling failures.

The tour Michaelson succeeded in arranging was a direct result of the demise of the Chamber Symphony of Philadelphia in the fall of 1968. The Philadelphia group had committed to an extensive February tour beginning in New Mexico and concluding at New York's Carnegie Hall, but the orchestra's dissolution put an end to those plans. Michaelson stepped in and booked the SPCO in the Philadelphia ensemble's place. Suddenly and unexpectedly, Sipe and his new full-time orchestra were preparing for an appearance on one of the music world's biggest stages. "This was do or die," cellist Eddie Blitz recalled. "You come up to the plate ... if you don't get a hit, you get the lockers, pack up your bag and go home."

The Carnegie Hall concert on February 20, 1969, was a typical Sipe program: two modern works (the American premiere of Hans Werner Henze's *Kammerkonzert* and the New York premiere of Joseph Ott's *Matrix III*); a Baroque piece (Telemann's Suite in F); and two classical favorites (Mozart's Symphony No. 29 in A major, K. 201, and Haydn's Symphony No. 99 in G). Sipe and his musicians believed they played their best, but had no idea how the New York critics would react. When the concert was over, Sipe and his family hopped in a taxi and, in a scene reminiscent of a Hollywood movie, asked the driver to show them around town until the first editions of the newspapers hit the stands. "The cab driver was just as excited as we were," Elaine Sipe recalled. "He stopped the cab and just listened to the review." Leopold Sipe opened the *New York Times* and read the opening paragraph of the review by critic Donal Henahan.

The SPCO's 1969 concert at Carnegie Hall was one of the high points of Leopold Sipe's career.

> *The conversion of St. Paul, so to speak, from an appendage of Minneapolis into a strong artistic partner is obviously well advanced, if last night's concert at Carnegie Hall is a fair test. Leopold Sipe put his St. Paul Chamber Orchestra through a program that would have strained the talent of any such organization, and brought it off most successfully.*

After toiling for years in Midwestern obscurity, Sipe had finally forced some of the toughest critics in the country to acknowledge the superior music his orchestra was making. Unfortunately, many other aspects of his relationship with the SPCO were, at the same time, turning sour.

The End of the Beginning

During its first ten years, The Saint Paul Chamber Orchestra had undergone a remarkable transformation. From a part-time ensemble made up almost entirely of Minneapolis Symphony musicians, the SPCO had turned itself into the nation's only full-time, community-funded chamber orchestra. Average attendance had grown from about 125 to approximately a thousand. Its resume included a well-received album and an appearance at Carnegie Hall. Its future seemed limitless—but financially, it was a mess.

Female professional musicians were still something of a novelty in 1967 when the *St. Paul Pioneer Press* profiled the women of the SPCO in an article titled, "Chamber Orchestra Displays Feminine Charm." Left to right: Susan Matthew, Arlene Halverson, Mary Roberts Wilson, Cynthia Eddy Britt, Rose Marie Johnson, Maxine Elworthy, and Judith Yanchus.

The SPCO had never been a moneymaker. Its first season produced a $2,000 deficit eliminated only by extra contributions from Philharmonic Society board members.

Since then, revenue—supplied primarily by contributions from the Arts Council—had never managed to cover expenses. The switch to full-time musicians only exacerbated the problem. During the 1967-1968 season, when the orchestra introduced its nine-player resident core, expenses nearly quadrupled from almost $50,000 to $190,000. The following year, when the entire orchestra went full-time, the annual budget was in the $300,000 range. The Arts Council had boosted its contributions to the SPCO over the years, but the increases didn't come close to keeping up with the orchestra's ballooning expenses.

The SPCO was not the only American orchestra facing a financial crisis. Orchestras throughout the country had expanded during the 1960s, extending their seasons, adding administrative staff, and sweetening musicians' contracts. Between 1961 and 1970, the expenditures of twenty-eight major American orchestras had increased nearly 200 percent. But revenues had failed to keep up, rising only 137 percent during the same period. Predictions that the growing middle class would support expanded orchestral programs proved to be wildly optimistic; it was hard to find an orchestra anywhere that wasn't in financial trouble.

In February 1969, while Sipe and his musicians were in New Mexico on the first leg of the tour that would conclude at Carnegie Hall, Philharmonic Society President Donald Wolkoff sent a letter—by priority air mail—to Sipe and each of the SPCO's twenty-one musicians. The letter informed the players that the orchestra faced a financial crisis and under the advice of the Arts Council, their contracts would not be renewed until new funding was secured. Sipe's response to the Wolkoff and the Philharmonic board revealed his frustration.

The most bitter disappointment is that the Council people can't see the gem of true unique greatness germinating in their own front yard. They are not concerned enough to try to understand the orchestral field. All over the country [contract] renewals go out to musicians in the face of large deficits. The philosophy is: keep the good musicians ... we want them—and now let's take the proper steps to finance them. The timing is rarely convenient, but evidently this attitude keeps orchestras in business.

A few days later, during a meeting of the Philharmonic Society Board of Directors, board member Bob Gumnit moved that the society—and by extension, the orchestra—declare bankruptcy and disband. The motion failed to gain a second, but it highlighted a stark reality: Even as the SPCO prepared for its Carnegie Hall debut, it faced the possibility of imminent extinction.

The society managed to keep the orchestra afloat through a combination of bank loans and foundation grants, but other problems remained. Uncertainties about the orchestra's financial viability repeatedly delayed progress on a new musicians' contract during the spring and summer of 1969. As a result, several players resigned in disgust. The dispute over contracts was not the only source of frustration among the musicians; orchestra members were growing increasingly dissatisfied with their conductor.

Turtlenecks, ties, and cigars: SPCO musicians show off their eclectic style in this 1970-1971 publicity photo.

Leopold Sipe had proven his worth many times over since arriving in Saint Paul in 1959. Unlike "maestros" with impressive resumes and egos to match, Sipe had not confined his efforts exclusively to his orchestra. He spent countless hours building up other programs—the youth symphony, the summer camp, and the Civic Orchestra—that helped create a solid base of community support for the SPCO. He had always hoped to turn the chamber orchestra into something more than a good regional ensemble, but bided his time, patiently waiting for the Philharmonic board to accept his vision.

The SPCO's transformation into a full-time resident orchestra during the 1967-1968 and 1968-1969 seasons was the realization of Sipe's dreams, but it also marked the beginning of his downfall. Over the years, Sipe had developed a persnickety manner ("he was *very* particular about precision on instruments," flutist Mary Wilson said), which worked well with amateur and part-time musicians, but grated on highly skilled professionals. Violinist Carolyn Daws (later Carolyn Gunkler), who joined the SPCO in the summer of 1968, remembered how morale within the orchestra deteriorated as it dawned on Sipe that his old methods were no longer working.

As the orchestra became better and better, it became more demanding. The musicians were demanding artistic control and guarantees and certain conditions, and [Sipe] began to feel his ability to control it slip away. And as a result he became very aggressive as far as becoming defensive and possessive of the orchestra ... I do remember him coming into rehearsal and announcing that the orchestra was folding—it was done with, no more rehearsals until further notice—and just slamming the door and going, leaving us. And we all sat there saying, now what do we do?

Adding to Sipe's problems was a changing of the guard in the orchestra's management ranks. In March 1969—at the same time the Philharmonic board was struggling to save the SPCO from financial ruin—a young administrator from the Pittsburgh Symphony, Stephen Sell, took over as the Philharmonic Society's new general manager. Sipe initially lauded Sell as "one of the outstanding managers in the country," but the two men clashed nearly from the start. After almost single-handedly raising enough foundation money to balance the society's books, Sell turned his attention to the inner workings of the orchestra. He usurped Sipe's office and parking space. He forced Sipe's good friend Elaine Springsted to resign her long-held position as administrator of the summer camp. Sell had strong ideas about where the orchestra should go and did not much care whether Sipe agreed with him. "There was nothing I could do about it," Sipe recalled.

In the fall of 1970, Sell called the Philharmonic's new president, Gene Warlich, into his office and told him Leopold Sipe had to go. "We sat down and he said to me in relatively short order that if this orchestra was ever going to amount to anything, we had to make a change in the music director," Warlich recalled. "This took me by complete surprise." Warlich told Sell that he wouldn't agree to fire Sipe without conducting an investigation of his own.

Over the next three months, Warlich spoke with a variety of people inside and outside the organization to find out what they thought of Sipe. The responses he received were enlightening and disturbing. Most of the people he talked with believed that Sipe was no longer an effective leader. He came to rehearsals unprepared. He berated musicians. He patronized women. He showed little respect for his players and his players responded in kind. The word was that several key members of the orchestra would leave if Sipe stayed.

At a meeting on January 14, 1971, the Philharmonic Society Board of Directors voted to terminate Leopold Sipe as music director of The Saint Paul Chamber Orchestra. The vote was fourteen to two, with two abstentions.

As Sipe later told the story in his autobiography, Warlich called him into his office the next morning and told him of the board's decision. Warlich suggested that Sipe take a couple weeks off before publicly announcing that he was stepping down. Sipe agreed to hold off saying anything to the press, but insisted he would not step down from the podium until he had conducted a pair of scheduled concerts during the next two weeks.

"I didn't give [Warlich] the opportunity to shake my hand," Sipe wrote. "I left his office, closed the door very quietly and went home."

News of the firing leaked out a few days later, before Sipe had a chance to make a formal announcement. Articles in the Twin Cities newspapers quoted unnamed sources as saying the orchestra had "outgrown" Sipe and that the ensemble's morale had bottomed out. Since no one within the organization was speaking on the record, it wasn't clear whether Sipe would conduct the remaining concerts.

Reaction to the news was quick and vehement. Sipe's many admirers couldn't understand why the Philharmonic board was sacking the man who had brought the SPCO to its current position of near national prominence. "The termination by the board of Mr. Sipe's services as conductor of the St. Paul Chamber Orchestra is deplorable," wrote a reader of the *Saint Paul Dispatch*. "He has honed a jewel for St. Paul and it is a pity that the board doesn't recognize it."

The SPCO's performance at Stillwater State Prison during the 1968-1969 season was an unnerving experience for many of the musicians.

Sipe's final appearance as conductor of the SPCO (he appeared as a violin soloist two months later) took place the evening of January 24, 1971, before a capacity audience at the Crawford Livingston Theater. The guest soloist was the world-renowned flutist, Jean-Pierre Rampal. It was, Sipe later recalled, a night to remember.

> *The famous flutist was first on the program and walked onto the stage first. I followed. The audience rose to its feet with thunderous applause. I'm certain that it was the first concert Rampal had ever done and gotten a standing ovation before he blew a note. It tickled me, since I knew what the ovation was all about.*

Most members of the Philharmonic's board believed they had acted in the orchestra's best interest when they fired Sipe, but many of them regretted the way his dismissal played out. They knew Sipe deserved better than to have the news of his firing leaked to the press before he had a chance to make a public statement. More than that, he deserved proper credit for all the work he had done over the past twelve years.

Looking back on those early years, former Philharmonic Society President Larry Platt marveled at all the things Sipe had accomplished. "We needed a guy who could do a lot of things and was willing to do a lot of things," he said. "[We didn't need] a guy who was a prima donna, simply an orchestra conductor who wouldn't dirty his hands with anything else. Sipe was the guy we needed."

Leopold Sipe
Music Director, 1959-1971

Among the things that most Minnesotans did not know about Leopold Sipe was that his first name was not really Leopold; it was Melvin. Leopold was his middle name. Melvin Leopold Sipe Jr. never liked either of his given names, which was why he didn't mind that his relatives in the Carolinas, the people who knew him best, called him Bob to distinguish him from his identically named father. Melvin—or Bob, as the case might be—was able to virtually ignore his middle name until 1959, when he applied to become music director of the Saint Paul Philharmonic Society. The man interviewing him for the

job, Ralph Burgard, was not keen to have a Melvin or a Bob conducting the new Saint Paul Chamber Orchestra. He asked Sipe if he would mind using his middle name instead. The young conductor said he would be glad to oblige. Leopold Sipe got the job.

Sipe did not fit the mold of a typical conductor. Born September 3, 1924, in the town of Fountain Inn, South Carolina, he was a musical prodigy from a decidedly un-musical family. As far as he knew, his great-grandmother, a country fiddler, was the only musician his family had ever produced.

When Sipe was five years old, his father, the town's postmaster, bought him a $3.95 half-size violin with proceeds from the sale of a flock of backyard chickens. The youngster took to the instrument and before long was soaking up whatever instruction he could receive from a series of teachers with names like Lennie Lusbye, Claire Ordway, and Guillermo DeRoxlo (the director of North Carolina's Charlotte Symphony Orchestra). He excelled as a "fiddler" and also became proficient at clarinet and piano.

After graduating from high school in 1941, Sipe was unsure what to do with his musical gifts. He flunked out of Davidson College, landed a job at a lumberyard, and, with the nation at war, enlisted in the Navy. While in the service, he began to focus on the possibilities of a musical career. He was assigned to a Navy band and wound up playing clarinet beside some of the country's top swing band musicians (from the Jimmy and Tommy Dorsey bands, among others) and some equally accomplished orchestral players. He learned the art of arranging and notation, played chamber music with his string-playing buddies, and used weekend passes to attend big-city orchestra performances conducted by Arturo Toscanini, Bruno Walter, and Leopold Stowkowski. It was, he later recalled, "one of the greatest learning experiences of my life."

Sipe spent the last two years of the war in a military hospital, receiving treatment for tuberculosis, a disease from which he never fully recovered. After his discharge, he studied violin and conducting at the Eastman School of Music and—for one summer—

at Juilliard. He moved back to the Carolinas and turned a part-time position at the Charlotte Opera Company into a full-time music directorship. There he met and married a young soprano, Elaine McSwain. After a few years in Charlotte, the couple moved cross-country to Washington, where Sipe became conductor of the Tacoma Symphony. It was in Tacoma that he first heard about a job opening for a chamber orchestra conductor in Minnesota.

During his eleven years in Saint Paul, Sipe impressed nearly everyone he met with his easy-going Southern manner and his devotion to the chamber orchestra. During performances, his natural affability often gave way to a professional formality. Rarely a showman, his conducting was precise and controlled. He moved his baton only from the elbow to compensate for bursitis in his right shoulder.

Sipe adapted quickly to his new home in Saint Paul, but he never completely shed his small-town Southern ways. He smoked a corncob pipe. He showed up after hours at local taverns and played "old gypsy stuff" on his fiddle. His Carolina drawl was unmistakable.

Leopold Sipe faded into professional obscurity after losing his job with the SPCO in 1971. He had a short stint on the music faculty of Western Illinois University, then spent the next ten years as a professor at Kent State University. Only rarely did he conduct. At age fifty-six, with the respiratory problems caused by his wartime bout with tuberculosis worsening, Sipe retired to North Carolina, where he died in 1992. The following year, the SPCO commissioned Stanislaw Skowaczewski (who had taken over the Minneapolis Symphony Orchestra in 1960, shortly after Sipe first arrived in Saint Paul) to compose a piece—the *Chamber Concerto*—in honor of its first conductor.

Review

Gutche: *Bongo Divertimento*; Fetler: *Nothing but Nature*; Haydn: Symphony No. 73 in D ("The Hunt"); The Saint Paul Chamber Orchestra and the Hamline University College Choir, Leopold Sipe conducting.

The works by Gene Gutche and Paul Fetler were commissioned by the St. Paul ensemble. The Gutche divertimento is a refreshing little work, exploiting cleverly and without pretension the use of bongos and related instruments. It would make a superior score for a film cartoon. Mr. Fetler's work is a cantata based on a poem by Ogden Nash, rather over-elaborate and conventional in humor. The performances seem right, and the one of the Haydn symphony is admirably crispy and tidy. New music deserves exposure, and it is good that the St. Paul group not only commissions works but is recording them. More disks are promised for the future. The engineering, in stereo, is satisfactory.

—*New York Times*, April 26, 1964

Chapter Two
A New Era

———

Few members of the audience knew exactly what to expect as they settled back into their seats at the O'Shaughnessy Auditorium. The first half of The Saint Paul Chamber Orchestra's 1974-1975 season-opening program had featured two enjoyable and accessible works by American composers—John Frederick Peter's Quintetto II in A Major and Henry Cowell's *Persian Set*. The rest of the program, however, promised to be less predictable. The first piece following intermission was to be the premiere of a new work by the avant-garde composer, John Cage. Its unwieldy title—*Score (40 drawings by Thoreau) and 23 parts (for any instruments and/or voices): Twelve Haiku followed by a recording of the dawn at Stony Point, New York, August 6, 1974*—suggested that it wouldn't have much in common with Haydn's Symphony No. 6, which was scheduled to close out the evening.

It was probably a good thing that those concertgoers who had not yet warmed to the SPCO's young and adventurous conductor, Dennis Russell Davies, could not see the score he had placed on his music stand. It contained no notes to speak of, no sharps or flats, no bass or treble clefs. Instead, its pages were covered with reproductions of drawings by Henry David Thoreau—little animals, plants, and clouds—arranged in horizontal, segmented rows. The musicians' scores were even more perplexing—bizarre tableaus of lines, squiggles, dashes, and dots that looked even less decipherable than the doodles Davies had to work with.

The music that filled O'Shaughnessy for the next twelve minutes or so consisted of twelve clusters of atonal blips, spatters, twitters, starts, and glissandi, separated at regular intervals by walls of silence. Sometimes the musicians made sounds with their instruments. At other times, they used their hands or their feet or their voices. The audience became restless. Whispering wafted from the seats. Then came the second movement, a tape recording of ambient sound assembled by the composer—another twelve minutes of mostly white noise punctuated by birdsong and the whoosh of passing trucks.

Then it was over.

The audience roared to life in an outpouring of raucous ambivalence. For a few moments, O'Shaughnessy rang with the competing sounds of boos and bravos. Eventually, though, the applause won out. Cage, who had joined the orchestra onstage, displayed the equanimity of a composer who was used to mixed reviews.

Left: The SPCO's new music director, Dennis Russell Davies, resplendent in ruffles and burgundy.

Below: When the concert featuring John Cage's *Score* was complete, St. Paul Mayor Lawrence Cohen (left, at the microphone) joined Davies, General Manager James Howland, and Board President Marge Allen onstage to wish the orchestra bon voyage on its upcoming tour of Eastern Europe.

In the newspapers the next day, local critics reflected the audience's conflicted response to Cage's creation.

"The best that can be said," wrote the *Minneapolis Star's* Michael Anthony, "is that it compelled one's interest and that it was faithfully reproduced by Dennis Russell Davies and his players."

John Harvey of the *Saint Paul Pioneer Press* was more forgiving. "Make of all this what you will," he concluded after describing the piece's eccentricities. "Myself, I wouldn't have missed it."

A New Identity

The infusion of foundation money that saved the SPCO from financial ruin in the summer of 1969 came with strings attached. The largest contribution, $200,000, was from the Bush Foundation, one of the Twin Cities' leading philanthropic organizations. Although the Bush grant was well timed and much appreciated, its terms were limiting. The grant money was to be spent mostly on outreach—programs that took music out of the concert hall and into the community—not to pay down the orchestra's mounting deficit or to cover its regular operating expenses.

The orchestra's new general manager, Stephen Sell, was happy to accommodate the Bush Foundation in its efforts to encourage arts outreach. Like many of his contemporaries, Sell believed that orchestras needed to actively seek out new audiences in unexpected places. He was convinced that the SPCO was in an enviable position to do just that. "As society becomes more impersonal and mechanized, the need grows greater for smaller, more personal aesthetic experiences," he wrote. "Because of its small size and the resultant mobility and flexibility, a chamber orchestra is uniquely able to provide these experiences." Adding to the orchestra's flexibility was the new musicians' contract, which made it possible to break the group into small ensembles that could cover more ground.

The SPCO's "Music on the Move" truck became a symbol of the orchestra's new commitment to musical outreach.

The Philharmonic Society had always considered outreach an important part of its mission (the Civic Orchestra, the youth symphony, and the summer camp were, in many respects, extension programs designed to build public awareness and appreciation of music), but Sell wanted the SPCO itself to become more involved in the community. With the funds from the Bush grant in hand, he set out to remake and repackage the orchestra's outreach efforts.

The result was "Music on the Move," a collection of new initiatives that put the SPCO's vaunted flexibility on full display. The orchestra made itself available for one-week residencies at colleges and communities outside the Twin Cities metro area. (Alexandria was the first town to host an SPCO residency in 1970.) It visited local schools to present concerts and instruct both students and teachers. It played joint concerts with church choirs. Funds provided by the Bush Foundation subsidized all Music on the Move events and allowed sponsors to bring in the SPCO for as little as a third of the actual cost.

Sell recognized the marketing potential of a good brand name and he soon began introducing new programs and events to fit under the Music on the Move umbrella. He called the woodwind quintet's free outdoor, lunch-hour concerts "Sandwich Serenades." He repeatedly dispatched the orchestra's twenty-two musicians to twenty-two different schools and dubbed the events "22 in 22." In a subtle marketing strategy that would confuse the historical record for years to come, he began referring to 1969 as the year the SPCO was founded (thus negating Leopold Sipe's ten years of work). Sell was creating a new identity for the orchestra—one built largely on its outreach efforts— and critics around the country were taking notice. "These activities make [the SPCO] one of the most important music groups in the country," the *New York Times'* Raymond Ericson wrote. "It may set the pattern for similar organizations, especially those in danger of extinction."

A "Sandwich Serenade" outside the Saint Paul Arts and Science Center in the summer of 1971.

Despite the SPCO's early success with Music on the Move, extinction remained a distinct possibility. The Bush Foundation grant lasted only through the 1970-1971 season and, even with that extra money, the orchestra faced a projected deficit topping $100,000. The SPCO needed new underwriters, and it needed to find them quickly.

Ever since his arrival in St. Paul in the spring of 1969, Stephen Sell had been working to raise the orchestra's profile with some of the nation's biggest charitable givers, especially the Ford Foundation. A meeting with Ford Foundation representatives had convinced him that the foundation was eager to shift its attention away from big symphony orchestras (which its directors deemed uninterested in community service) to smaller ensembles like the SPCO. Seeing a potentially lucrative opening, Sell pressed his case with the foundation, making sure to take advantage of the positive press the Music on the Move program was generating both locally and nationally.

On April 15, 1971, Philharmonic Society President Eugene Warlich called a news conference to announce what amounted to a life-saving development. The SPCO had secured pledges totaling more than $1 million from the Ford Foundation (which accounted for nearly half the total) and five local philanthropies—the Bush Foundation, the Hill Family Foundation, the First National Bank of Saint Paul, the Burlington Northern Foundation, and the orchestra's most reliable partner, the Saint Paul Council of Arts and Sciences. Spread out over three years, the new infusion of cash promised to stabilize the orchestra's perennially shaky finances. Much, if not most, of the credit for landing the grants rightfully belonged to Stephen Sell, and Sell was relieved that his efforts had paid off. "The partnership of these national and local philanthropies in this program is a very gratifying endorsement of our chamber orchestra concept," he wrote. "But more important is the challenge it embodies to assure financial stability for the Orchestra's future."

The orchestra's finances had indeed stabilized, but its artistic prospects remained uncertain. Sell had managed to convince the Philharmonic board to fire Leopold Sipe just three months earlier. Associate Conductor Edouard Forner stepped in to complete the 1970-1971 season, but it wasn't clear whether Forner would get the chance to become the Philharmonic Society's full-time music director. Sipe's dismissal had created a leadership vacuum on the podium and filling that vacuum promised to be a time consuming proposition.

New Kid in Town

The 1971-1972 season was among the most difficult the musicians of the SPCO had ever experienced. "It was terrible," harpsichordist Layton "Skip" James recalled years later. "It was like being a pickup orchestra." Sell had arranged for ten conductors (including Edouard Forner) to lead the SPCO during the course of the season and nearly every one of them was considered a candidate for the open music director job. Each concert was to be, in essence, a tryout.

The parade of conductors included several impressive candidates. Among the favorites were Leonard Slatkin, associate conductor of the Saint Louis Symphony Orchestra; Michael Charry, assistant conductor of the Cleveland Orchestra; and composer-pianist-conductor Lukas Foss.

The last candidate added to the list was perhaps the most unlikely of them all. Dennis Russell Davies, a twenty-seven-year-old product of Juilliard, felt lucky even to be considered. At the time he received the invitation, he was conducting *Rigoletto* in San Francisco—the first job he'd held in three months. He was known primarily as a modern music specialist who had conducted several world premieres, including Luciano Berio's *Opera* in Santa Fe, New Mexico, and Hall Overton's *Huckleberry Finn* at the American Opera Center in New York. He had co-founded the Ensemble (formerly the Juilliard Ensemble), a respected group of sixteen musicians dedicated to the performance of new and recent works. He also was an accomplished pianist.

Three of the five pieces Davies selected for his SPCO debut were 20th century compositions—Goffredo Petrassi's *Estri*, Neil McKay's *Kaleidoscope*, and Stravinsky's *Ragtime*. (Haydn and Beethoven rounded out the program.) Davies believed his audition concert on January 9, 1972, went well, but the reviews were mixed. The write-up in the University of Minnesota newspaper, the *Minnesota Daily*, suggested that Davies had left his audience perplexed.

At intermission there is widespread apprehension. Nervous patrons whisper, "Is it safe for us to be here?" "Do they know what they are doing?" "What kind of madness is this crazy Petrassi music anyway?" At the same time there are defiant remarks of "Glorious! Incredible!" "Even here in St. Paul, the music of modern civilization can be heard!" "This conductor is one to trust. He knows what he is doing."

The reaction from the orchestra was overwhelmingly positive. About a week after the concert, Sell called to tell Davies that he appeared to be the frontrunner and that he "ought to be thinking about coming out here." The musicians voted among themselves to recommend Davies and made their preference known to the Philharmonic's board. When the final votes were counted, Dennis Russell Davies was the unanimous choice to become The Saint Paul Chamber Orchestra's second music director.

Stephen Sell was delighted with the choice. In Davies he had a young, dynamic conductor, oozing with public relations potential. If nothing else, he looked nothing like the stuffy, penguin-suited conductors many people associated with classical music. His wispy, shoulder-length hair swept back from a severely receding hairline. At about five-foot-five, he was much shorter than his predecessor, the lanky Leopold Sipe. He wore T-shirts and jeans and boots. He smiled easily. As one reporter later put it, he looked like "an impish Hell's Angel."

Sell wasted little time constructing a publicity campaign around his new conductor. He deluged reporters with stories about Davies's background, family, and hobbies—especially motorcycles and baseball. (Davies was a Detroit Tigers fan, but was willing to transfer his loyalties to the Minnesota Twins.) He put Davies's face on the sides of MTC buses. He had Davies's voice radio spots to run on the rock and roll station, KQRS. He also launched a pair of brash new slogans. The first one—"Dennis Russell Davies came to play. So did The Saint Paul Chamber Orchestra"—put Davies front and center. The second—"Come Hear Minnesota's Other Great Orchestra"—was an awkward attempt to contrast the SPCO with the recently renamed Minnesota Orchestra (the former Minneapolis Symphony). In a planning document produced in the months leading up to Davies's first season with the orchestra, Sell could hardly contain his enthusiasm. "It is difficult to imagine a finer set of credentials than those Mr. Davies brings to the position," he wrote. "We must work vigorously to make him known, but there is a great deal to work with."

The iconic image of Dennis Russell Davies during his first year on the job. One reporter described the SPCO's new music director as "an impish Hell's Angel."

Great Leap Forward

Five years earlier, during the SPCO's first season as a full-time, professional orchestra, the women of the ensemble had begun appearing onstage in "costumes" described by longtime board member Elaine Springsted as "femininely attractive but not distracting." When the orchestra under Dennis Russell Davies debuted on October 14, 1972, at the College of Saint Catherine's new O'Shaughnessy Auditorium, everyone in the orchestra—not just the women—was wearing a "costume." This time, the sartorial switch was hard to ignore.

As the orchestra took the stage, the audience, already anticipating what was being billed as a "great leap forward" in the SPCO's development, began murmuring with excitement and, in some cases, amusement. The players were wearing suits and dresses of blue velvet. The longhaired conductor was in a contrasting wine-colored outfit complete with ruffled shirt and big bow tie. The days of Leopold Sipe were definitely over.

Everything about the SPCO suddenly seemed new. The conductor, the onstage outfits, the concertmaster—Davies's Juilliard friend Romuald Tecco, the stylish

Dennis Russell Davies and Assistant Conductor John DeMain model their new "costumes."

inspiration behind the blue suits, and the concert hall (the O'Shaughnessy was the SPCO's first acoustically reliable home). "This is the year The Saint Paul Chamber Orchestra answers the big question, the sink-or-swim question," Davies said. "We are definitely poised on the edge of a new era here and we're going to take the jump."

The program for the debut concert at the O'Shaughnessy reflected Davies's vision for the orchestra. The first half began with American composer Charles Ives's Symphony No. 3 and concluded with Ralph Vaughan Williams's *Concerto Accademico*. After intermission came the premiere of Max Lifchitz's *Roberta* and a Mozart finale (Symphony No. 40 in G minor). It was an eclectic program—heavy on 20th-century works—that challenged both the orchestra and the audience. *Minneapolis Star* critic Peter Altman felt both the orchestra and audience rose to the challenge.

Davies and his players clearly realized that their debut concert represented a big opportunity to make a mark, and were extraordinarily charged up. A special crackle of excitement was in the air, [as was] a sense of pride and self-assertion that chamber orchestra events in the past have lacked ...

One successful concert doesn't make a great musical organization. But Saturday's lively and appealing program certainly got the chamber orchestra's hoped for "new era" off to an auspicious start.

The size of the audience that night constituted yet another leap forward for the orchestra; the crowd of 1,400 was the largest ever to attend an SPCO subscription concert. The move into the spacious O'Shaughnessy was a major factor in attracting the big audience, but a change in ticket policy was just as crucial.

In the year and a half since the firing of Leopold Sipe, attendance at SPCO concerts dropped precipitously. The size of the average crowd during the 1971-1972 guest-conductor season had declined to about four hundred and season ticket sales had plummeted nearly 40 percent from their Sipe-era peak. A marketing plan drawn up by Stephen Sell during the summer of 1972 identified shrinking ticket sales as the most dangerous threat to the SPCO's future and predicted that the downward trend would "certainly spell doom unless it [could] be reversed." Sell suggested that the orchestra adopt a new marketing strategy focused on attracting large audiences—even if it meant selling tickets at bargain basement prices. From now on, he wrote, the main goal should be "filling the house." Sell believed that a new policy aimed at

The "new look" Saint Paul Chamber Orchestra of the early 1970s.

maximizing attendance not only would produce more earned income, it would attract big donors. "Foundations predicate their grants upon evidence of public interest and the appeal of an enterprise," he concluded. "Indeed, there is just no point in playing if no one comes to hear."

Under Sell's new ticket policy, students, military personnel, and senior citizens who were willing to wait until fifteen minutes before a performance could purchase leftover balcony seat tickets for whatever price they wanted to pay. The pay-what-you-can approach appealed especially to cash-strapped college students, and was a significant factor in attracting the record-setting crowd that attended the debut concert at the O'Shaughnessy. "When I came on stage the orchestra and I sort of looked up and saw that there were 1,100 people in the balcony, predominantly young," Davies said. "Downstairs we had the large number of very traditional concertgoers ... [It was] probably one of the broadest cross-sections of a public that the Twin Cities [had] seen in one hall in a long time."

As the season progressed and word spread of the SPCO's new blue-velvet ways, big crowds became the norm (attendance at the O'Shaughnessy averaged about 1,200) and audiences continued to skew younger. "The audience seems a little different from the usual Minnesota Orchestra audience," one reporter noted. "The Kenwood social bunch is missing, of course; there are fewer furs in general, and many more tennies." Season ticket sales continued to languish, but the fill-the-house strategy was at least putting people in the seats.

As in past seasons, the 1972-1973 subscription concerts were divided into series. Under Davies there were two of them: the Capital Series, at the O'Shaughnessy, which epitomized the orchestra's standard mix of Baroque, Classical, and Modern; and the Perspectives Series, at the Walker Arts Center in Minneapolis, which focused exclusively on New Music. Even more than the performances at the O'Shaughnessy, the Perspectives programs at the Walker attracted young concertgoers who typically avoided any art form associated with their parents' generation. They enjoyed listening to music and chatting with the players in a casual, intimate setting. The musicians seemed to enjoy the programs just as much as the audience. "It was terrific," Skip James said. "Very often we'd all meet somewhere over in Minneapolis and drink and talk about the music even more afterward."

Davies structured the season so that the Perspectives Series and the Capital Series worked in tandem. During the 1972-1973 season, both series relied heavily on music by two very different composers—the late 17th-century Italian Arcangelo Corelli and American Charles Ives. (In subsequent seasons Davies would pair Bach with Stravinsky and Haydn with Cage.) The goal, Davies explained, was to create "a very surprising experience."

> *A good concert, programmed with both old and new music can be a wonderful creative experience—and not just for those of us playing the music but for the people hearing it. We want to demonstrate that experience and once we do we feel our audience will grow and respond enthusiastically. In any case, that's our approach—to stretch the limits of our audience at the same time we're stretching our own abilities.*

Movable

In the summer of 1973, about a year after Davies joined the SPCO, Stephen Sell left Saint Paul for a new position with the National Endowment for the Arts. (He would go on to serve in high-ranking executive positions with the National Endowment for the Arts, the Minnesota State Arts Board, the Atlanta Symphony, and the Philadelphia Orchestra.) During his four-and-a-half years with the Philharmonic Society, Sell had put the orchestra on sound financial footing (at least in the short term), introduced the successful Music on the Move concept, and brought in a dynamic new conductor. He also had set in motion another initiative that would not reach fruition until he was gone. Although few people realized it, he had paved the way for the SPCO to go international.

In 1969, during his first few months on the job, Sell had approached the U.S. State Department to find out whether the federal government would be willing to send the SPCO on an overseas tour. His pitch was simple and it hinged on basic economics: The cost of sending a chamber orchestra abroad would be far less than the cost of underwriting a symphony orchestra tour. Sell's contacts at the State Department liked the idea of turning the musicians of the SPCO into goodwill ambassadors, but the federal bureaucracy moved slowly. Sell continued pushing the proposal throughout his tenure with the Philharmonic Society, but the State Department kept putting him off. He left Saint Paul without ever getting an answer.

James Howland, who replaced Sell, was determined to pick up where his predecessor left off. He believed an international tour would, among other things, help the SPCO distinguish itself from its larger counterpart on the other side of the Mississippi River. He knew that the Minnesota Orchestra had toured nationally for years. "What they hadn't done," he said, "was to do a major tour abroad." Howland reestablished contact with the State Department and discovered that the Nixon administration—mired as it was in Vietnam and Watergate—was eager to burnish its image wherever it could. Suddenly a goodwill tour by a group of fresh-faced American musicians sounded like a really good idea. "[The administration] had a lot of interest in having a presence in Eastern Europe," Howland recalled.

In the spring of 1974, Howland announced that the State Department was sending the SPCO on a three-week tour of countries behind what was commonly known as the Iron Curtain—Poland, Czechoslovakia, Yugoslavia, and Romania. The tour would take place the following autumn. It was the first time since the 1968 Soviet crackdown in Czechoslovakia that the U.S. government had agreed to sponsor a cultural presentation in Eastern Europe. It was also the first time it had arranged to send a chamber orchestra on an international tour.

The SPCO's tour of Eastern Europe in November 1974 was anything but glamorous. The musicians traveled from city to city by bus. Hotel accommodations were often much less inviting than advertised. Luggage and instruments took unexpected detours. ("Twice we took off in airplanes while the harpsichord and our wardrobe remained behind on the runway," Davies reported.) The musicians often arrived at their destination with barely enough time to wash up and eat before their next performance. Still, many of them considered the tour a highlight of their professional lives.

The SPCO made its international debut during a tour of Poland, Czechoslovakia, Yugoslavia, and Romania in the fall of 1974.

Davies and his orchestra had prepared four programs, each featuring a mix of the old (Haydn, Bach, Schubert) and the new (premieres of John Cage's latest work and a commissioned piece by Louis Ballard, *Incident at Wounded Knee*). The musicians played to overflow crowds and were overwhelmed by the response. "We had to play encore after encore," Concertmaster Romuald Tecco said. "Finally we would just run out of pieces to play. Then it was signing autographs, Dennis, all of us. We would keep signing, sometimes for half an hour. They would come back during intermission. It was like being Mick Jagger."

General Manager James Howland traveled with the orchestra during much of the tour and did everything he could to maximize the trip's public relations value. "We saw it as a strategic positioning thing," he explained. "We needed a triumphant European tour." Since no local reporters were covering the orchestra's travels, Howland fed photographs, stories, and reviews—"which may have been a little biased," he admitted—to the wire services. On its return home, the orchestra played a hurriedly staged welcome-back concert before a nearly packed house at the O'Shaughnessy. The program began with a slide show of the tour narrated by Davies. When the slide show was over, the lights came up, and the orchestra took the stage through a scrim of flags representing each of the countries visited during the tour. "It was a very emotional night," Howland recalled. "I think the audience was sharing the same kind of pride that we felt in having come back from that tour."

Suddenly the SPCO, which over the years had struggled to book even a handful of tour stops east of the Mississippi, was something of an international phenomenon. The Eastern European jaunt led to a second State Department-sponsored tour—of the Soviet Union—in the late fall of 1975. The Soviet trip was, if anything, even less glamorous than the previous tour. The Russian audiences were just as appreciative as the ones in Poland and Yugoslavia, but some government apparatchiks remained noticeably unenthused. "There were little sabotages," violinist Carolyn Daws recalled. "We'd go in to rehearse in a hall and it would be forty degrees below zero. They wouldn't have had the heat on for two days and, I mean, they knew we were coming. Janitors would all be wearing gloves and we were supposed to perform."

With its international touring credentials established, the SPCO shifted its attention to destinations closer to home. Although Howland believed the overseas appearances had left the SPCO's local and international reputations in "superb condition," he worried about its national image. "With respect to the national scene," he wrote, "we're in rather disastrous condition."

The efforts to enhance the SPCO's national reputation began in December 1974—a few weeks after the orchestra's return from Eastern Europe—with a mid-American tour

The SPCO's "movable" musicians traveled by bus when the concert venue was not too far from the Twin Cities. For destinations farther afield, the orchestra often squeezed into a chartered DC-3 airliner.

including stops in Kansas, Oklahoma, and Nebraska. The following season the orchestra beefed up its regional touring schedule with two one-week "home city" residencies in Northfield, Minnesota, and Bismarck, North Dakota. In all, the orchestra spent more than a third of its season on the road. "We'll play anywhere," exclaimed David Haskin, the new president of the Philharmonic's board. "It's another unique thing about us: we're movable."

If the destination wasn't too far from home, the musicians traveled by bus. When a tour spanned longer distances, the orchestra often chartered a plane—an ancient, 1930s-era DC-3. Flying on a chartered DC-3 was less expensive than traveling on a commercial airliner, but flying on the cheap had its downside. The noisy old airplane had barely enough seats to accommodate the entire orchestra, so one of the players—cellist Daryl Skobba—volunteered to create a little extra room by assuming the duties normally assigned to a "stewardess." Skobba received the requisite training and earned the distinction of becoming what was almost certainly history's first and only designated chamber-orchestra flight attendant.

Dennis Russell Davies rejected the notion that a conductor was an authoritarian figure, separate from his orchestra; on tour, he preferred to ride with his players. He blended seamlessly into his ensemble and his unassuming manner sometimes caused confusion. When the orchestra arrived in a new town, the welcoming delegation—looking to greet the conductor—often mistakenly headed for the orchestra's invariably well-dressed cellist, Eddie Blitz. "Ed was the one who looked like a conductor, not me," Davies explained. "There were a number of times when they went up [to Blitz] and said, 'Hello, Mr. Davies,' and he pointed to the kid over there with the long hair and the jeans and said, 'That's our music director.'"

By the end of the 1975-1976 season, Davies and the orchestra were exhausted. In two years, they had firmly established their credentials as musicians of local, national, and international repute. Nearly everywhere they went, the reviews were glowing. But traveling was hard work. One reporter exclaimed that the "list of the orchestra's recent tour destinations reads like a AAA road atlas"—twenty states and seventy-five cities. The musicians—especially the cello and bass players—were getting tired of lugging around their bags and instruments. They needed a break. "One of the things we want to do is to find more ways of being of more use here at home," Davies told a reporter with the *Saint Paul Pioneer Press*. "We've been away for large chunks of time. Next season we won't be making any big tours and we'll be around here a lot more."

Tumultuous Times

Ever since its creation in 1959, the SPCO had been just one component—albeit the most important one—of the Saint Paul Philharmonic Society. In the years since it had become a full-time professional ensemble, the links between it and the other components—the Civic Orchestra and the Philharmonic's youth program—had frayed. The society had ended its popular summer music camp in 1973 and by the summer of 1975 it had severed its last ties with the Civic Orchestra and the remnants of the old Youth Orchestra. (The Youth Orchestra split into two groups after the Sipe firing.) The jettisoning of the Civic Orchestra and the youth program left the SPCO as the only component under the Philharmonic umbrella. That fall, in recognition of the new reality, the Philharmonic Society officially changed its name to The Saint Paul Chamber Orchestra Society. SPCO board members hoped the name change would prevent further "confusion among the public." Unfortunately, it did nothing to address an even bigger problem—money.

The foundation grants that rescued the SPCO from financial ruin in 1971 had run out in 1974. Since then, funds had been increasingly tight. The specter of the return of large deficits forced the orchestra to lay off all its employees for three to five weeks in

May 1975. Strong ticket sales boosted by the orchestra's soaring artistic reputation had helped slow the financial bleeding, but everyone knew better box office could not by itself stave off looming deficits. The orchestra needed to find new sources of funds.

In the summer of 1976, the SPCO finally got some good financial news: The Ford Foundation came through with another major grant. Combined with matching contributions from Ramsey County, the Bush Foundation, and the McKnight Foundation, the Ford grant created a cash reserve fund of $350,000. But it wasn't enough.

Over the next several months, many of the programs the orchestra was counting on to generate income during the 1976-1977 season fell through. Plans for a major tour of western states—complete with underwriting—collapsed. A residency program at five local private colleges failed to materialize. Regional home cities including Bemidji, Northfield, and Bismarck were unable to raise the funds needed to cover the program's cost. By the end of the season, operational costs had wiped out the SPCO's cash reserve. The orchestra headed into the 1977-1978 season with a projected deficit of nearly $200,000. "We had a lot of luck for a long time," Davies said, looking back on that period. "I think there were a couple instances in that season where the luck ran out."

The return of budget deficits was just one of several signs that the SPCO was entering a period of upheaval. Davies had previously announced that he planned to take a leave of absence during the 1978-1979 season, but in May 1978, he went even further, announcing that he intended to leave the orchestra when his contract ran out in the spring of 1980. Davies had recently taken on several part-time conducting positions in Europe—most notably with the Stuttgart Opera—and now he was anxious to see where that career path might lead. "I had thought I could juggle my responsibilities to the Chamber Orchestra with my European career," he said. "I've come to the conclusion that I can't anymore."

Davies's decision coincided with—and perhaps helped trigger—a series of significant changes in the way the orchestra was managed and led. About an hour after Davies announced his plans to resign, the SPCO Executive Committee voted to fire James Howland. The full board endorsed the committee's action, citing Howland's inability to control the orchestra's budget deficit (it had grown to $250,000) and "a general loss of [faith] in the Executive Director's ability."

Although they did not say so publicly, some board members also had grown weary of Howland's close friendship with Arts Council President Marlow Burt. The Arts Council's financial support of the SPCO had steadily declined in recent years, and there was a widespread concern on the board that Howland and Burt's friendship might actually be hurting the orchestra rather than helping it. Even Howland recognized that his relationship with Burt was a problem. "We were way too close, no question about it," he later admitted. "The fact that Marlow Burt and I were drinking buddies ... added a lot of fuel to that fire."

The 1978-1979 season was a time of transition and tumult. Howland was gone. Davies took off on his sabbatical, leaving Jorge Mester, music director of the Louisville

[Kentucky] Symphony, to take over the podium. Word of a new record deficit—$447,000—fueled rumors that the SPCO would either fold or move to Houston, Texas. "Things have been changing so fast," *Minneapolis Tribune* music critic Michael Anthony wrote of the SPCO, "[that] it's been hard to keep up."

Change was underway on the board as well. The SPCO had never benefited from the kind of high-powered, deep-pocketed board leadership that the Minnesota Orchestra—with names such as Pillsbury, Musser, Lund, and Piper among its board members—enjoyed.

Students at Saint Paul's Pratt Elementary School get a taste of professional music-making from the SPCO's traveling wind ensemble, 1976.

The comparatively low profile of the SPCO board, when combined with longstanding fundraising restrictions imposed by the Arts Council, had made it difficult to build relationships in the Twin Cities business community. In a report prepared prior to the 1978-1979 season, the SPCO's Long Range Planning Committee spelled out the problem: If the board wished to stabilize the orchestra's "financial underpinnings," the committee concluded, it would have to begin "attracting additional members of the business community who have 'clout' and persons who have 'access' to wealth."

That fall, the board began actively recruiting the kind of well-connected people described in the committee's report. It wasn't long before its recruitment efforts started showing results. Topping the list of board additions was the retired president of Hoerner Waldorf Corp., John Myers, a tireless fundraiser who, in the words of *Saint Paul Pioneer Press* critic, Roy Close, "lent instant credibility" to the organization. Under Myers's leadership, the board launched a new fund drive with an audacious goal: $1.25 million. It hired a development director, Julie Duke, formerly with the Chicago Symphony, to coordinate the effort.

Duke invited Twin Cities business leaders to a series of fundraising luncheons at which she described the orchestra's financial crisis in stark terms. "[We] told them that what we needed right now was for them to put their support behind us," she said. "And the Saint Paul business community, I think much to the surprise of a lot of people—including themselves—did it." Three foundations and thirty-eight local businesses responded to the call. By the end of the 1978-1979 season, the SPCO's fund drive had surpassed its goal.

Rehearsal with Dennis Russell Davies conducting. Front Row: Romuald Tecco, Hanley Daws, and Daryl Skobba. Back Row: Juan Cuneo and Bruce Allard.

Bowing Out

With all the financial convulsions the SPCO had just endured, many of the orchestra's most ardent supporters assumed that Dennis Russell Davies would decline to return, as promised, for the 1979-1980 season. But Davies did return, refreshed after a year's sabbatical in Vermont, and he was determined to make his final season in Saint Paul a memorable one. "I've had the last year to think about my last dance and how I'm going to dance it," he said. "This year's programs and format are something I believe in very much."

In many ways, the musical choices that Davies made during his swan song season were similar to those he had always made. Through his pairings of composers from different eras—Henze and Scarlatii, Vivaldi and Ives, Bartók and Cage—he continued to explore what he called "the familiar threads between new and old." But his year in Vermont and the knowledge that he was entering his last season in Saint Paul seemed to free him from whatever remaining inhibitions he had about programming. The season was notable for several performances that solidified his reputation as a foremost champion of New Music.

On the evening Saturday, February 23, 1980, the SPCO presented the sixth concert in its Capital Series at O'Shaughnessy Auditorium. The program began with Mozart's Concerto in E-flat Major for Two Pianos and closed with two pieces by Mendelssohn— *The Hebrides* and Piano Concerto No. 1 in G Minor. In between came the world premiere of *Music for Every Occasion*, by avant-garde composer Alvin Curran. It was the Curran piece that everyone remembered.

Curran's instructions to the orchestra hinted at what the performance would entail. The horn players, equipped with a high-hat and a bass drum, would double as percussionists. The pianist was to play an "out-of-tune upright" and an "in-tune small grand." Curran—who planned to participate in the performance—needed a grand piano (in tune), a set of chimes, a microphone, an amplifier, a tape player, and a two-channel mixer. The entire piece would last approximately forty-five minutes.

As *Saint Paul Pioneer Press* critic David Hawley later described it, *Music for Every Occasion* was "a suite of songs, seven in number, tied together in one very long, swirling cloud of sound." Hawley found parts of the piece "enormously intriguing" and "sensuously beautiful," but, as he admitted in his review: "I suspect my opinion is in the minority, considering the audience's general reaction to the performance."

Over the years, Davies had challenged Twin Cities concertgoers to open their minds and ears to New Music. He had programmed works by more than fifty modern composers and had commissioned more than two dozen original pieces. He understood that many members of his audience found it difficult to fathom some of the music he chose, but always admired their willingness try something new. "The Twin Cities is the most important community of its kind in the country," he said. "It is one place where contemporary music and avant-garde artists have been brought into the mainstream of artistic activity." Only on rare occasions (the performance of John Cage's *Score* in 1974 was one example) did SPCO audiences express their displeasure with a new and challenging piece of music. Still, Curran's *Music for Every Occasion* was more than many concertgoers were willing to accept.

The accounts of what happened in the O'Shaughnessy that evening differed in their details. The *Minneapolis Tribune's* Michael Anthony wrote only that "a mood of restlessness" came over crowd as the Curran piece progressed. Kathy Grandchamp of the *Minneapolis Star* quoted the mutterings of miffed concertgoers. ("Dammit, Edith, you forgot to bring the earplugs.") David Hawley of the *Pioneer Press* provided the most detailed play-by-play.

A significant number of patrons stomped out during the piece, and it was interrupted once by derisive applause. Several people stood up and let their feelings be known at its conclusion, one standing directly in front of the podium and signaling a thumbs down, like Nero calling for the coup de grace ... Particular disdain was expressed for Curran's solo cadenza, a 10-minute affair that involved a shimmering, texture-exploring pattern on the piano, and Curran's singing—a sound akin to long, wailing Indian prayer calls.

The audience's reaction to the Curran piece—and a similar reaction a few weeks later to a performance of Arnold Schoenberg's *Pierrot Lunaire*—fed a growing sense that the time had come for Davies to move on. Many board members had begun to worry that Davies's adventurous programming appealed to young audiences with little disposable income—the "long hair crowd"—at the expense of older, more affluent patrons. The addition of a Baroque Series in 1975 helped mollify traditional concertgoers, but the Capital Series remained too daring for some people's taste. Grumbling among audience members was becoming more common and dissatisfaction was growing among the players as well. "It was frustrating because you took so much time to put this [contemporary music] together—you play it once and then it's gone," cellist Eddie Blitz explained. "As far as I'm concerned, some of the things we did did not warrant a second hearing."

During his years in Saint Paul, Davies had turned the SPCO into what critic David Hawley and others called "a world class organization." He had led the orchestra on successful international tours. He had, more than almost any other conductor in the country, championed the works of American composers. He had overseen the recording of several albums including one—a coupling of Aaron Copland's *Appalachian Spring* and Charles Ives's *Three Places in New England*—that won a Grammy Award just a few days after the controversial performance of the Alvin Curran piece. He had slowly expanded the orchestra to its current size of twenty-six players. Perhaps most impressively, he had achieved all these things without alienating himself from his musicians as Leopold Sipe had done a decade earlier. "We have become a very close-knit unit, and that's no accident" violist Sal Venittelli said. "This organization is right up there with any, [and] that is certainly the result of Dennis's work here."

Davies's last concert as music director of the SPCO, on May 17, 1980, was a love fest that began with a standing ovation. In a sign that the Davies era was ending, the players appeared in ordinary dresses and

Dennis Russell Davies celebrates the SPCO's first Grammy Award with representatives of the 3M Company (including CEO Lewis Lehr, far left), Sound 80 co-founder Herb Pilhofer (holding the album), and Minnesota Governor Al Quie (center). The SPCO recorded its renditions of Aaron Copland's *Appalachian Spring* and Charles Ives's *Three Places in New England* at Minneapolis's Sound 80 Studios, using 3M's prototype digital recording system.

business suits—their blue velvet wardrobe consigned to closets. The music—a typical Davies program featuring Ives, Vivaldi, and a premiere by Sidney Hodkinson—received enthusiastic applause, but was quickly overshadowed by everything that happened next. Amid raucous clapping and cheers, the children of some of the musicians toddled onstage to deliver bouquets to the conductor. Saint Paul Mayor George Latimer read a proclamation declaring "Molly and Dennis Russell Davies Day." (Davies was married to filmmaker Molly Davies.) Cellist Daryl Skobba presented Davies with a gift from the orchestra—a baseball bat, "suspiciously wrapped in blue velvet," with the message: "May you have as many hits with this as you have with us."

Davies thanked the orchestra and the audience, and left them with an admonition. "Take care of this orchestra," he said. "They are very special."

Davies's closing words hinted at the concerns he had for the SPCO as he left the podium. He had made it clear on more than one occasion that he took particular pride in creating programs that maintained a "reference point firmly anchored to music of our time." He worried that once he was gone, the orchestra's commitment to New Music would wane.

A year earlier, while Davies was still on sabbatical, the SPCO board had chosen Pinchas Zukerman to succeed him as music director. Zukerman was a violinist of breathtaking talent, but he was a novice conductor with little apparent love for contemporary music. The jump from Davies to Zukerman promised to be a formidable one, as Davies was well aware. "The constituency that supports [contemporary music] needs to realize … that it has some influence, that it can affect what is programmed here and who performs," he told a reporter during his last days in Saint Paul. "They need to organize themselves if this unique situation is to continue."

Dennis Russell Davies
Music Director, 1972-1980

Like many conductors, Dennis Russell Davies was most likely to reveal his true nature during rehearsals. Unlike many of his peers, Davies was not prone to throwing tantrums or berating musicians. "If there's something he feels needs a little ironing out, he might get a little stern," violinist Marti Sweet explained, "but he has a very even temperament."

Davies often showed up at rehearsals in blue jeans and cowboy boots, and the sessions tended to match his informal attire. He encouraged his musicians to ask questions when he did something that confused them, and he was willing to admit mistakes. In the fall of 1972—his first season with the SPCO—Davies invited *Minnesota Daily* reporter Jeff Holman to sit in on one of his rehearsals. In his story, Holman described a typical exchange between the conductor and his orchestra:

> *"Are you going to slow up at that section before C?"*
> *"Did it seem like I slowed up?"*
> *"Yeah."*
> *Davies is pensive.*
> *"It seemed like you rushed."*
> *The violins and the woodwinds laugh. They take C again.*
> *"We'll do this by feel," Davies says. "Just don't go like into a brick wall."*
> *They finish the section and Davies seems pleased. "Yes, right. I did slow down a little before that one."*

Although he was only twenty-eight when he took over the SPCO, Davies was already a confident and experienced pianist and conductor. A native of Toledo, Ohio, Davies had been making music as long as he could remember. He began playing piano at the age of three, started lessons a couple years later and, by his teens, was demonstrating so much talent that he was allowed to direct his high school band. He debuted as a pianist with the Toledo Symphony in 1965 and the following year was a finalist at the Busoni International Piano Competition. At Juilliard, he studied with pianists Lonny Epstein and Sasha Gorodnitzki, but soon developed an interest in conducting. "I have the kind of ear that can fit a large group of instruments together and make it work," he said. "After I found that it would work, it just seemed to interest me more and more."

During his years in Saint Paul, Davies impressed audiences and musicians alike with his crisp, almost technical conducting style. "Dennis was a master at beating time," violinist Carolyn Daws said. "He could beat two rhythms simultaneously—three with this hand and four with that."

Davies also was a generous music director who believed good communication between the conductor and the orchestra helped create an enjoyable evening for the audience. "Your audience likes to see rapport and I think they have a right to see it," he explained. "A good conductor is one who can respond to this [desire] and feels this rapport and longs to have it."

After leaving the SPCO in 1980, Davies forged a distinguished international career. He served as chief conductor with a host of orchestras, including the Stuttgart Chamber Orchestra, the Orchestra of the Beethovenhalle Bonn, the Vienna Radio Symphony Orchestra, the Bruckner Orchestra Linz, the Linz Opera, the Brooklyn Philharmonic, and the American Composers Orchestra (which he co-founded with composer Francis Thorne). In 2008, he was named music director of the Basel Symphony Orchestra in Switzerland. Still, even after years of receiving international acclaim, Davies continued to look back on his time in Saint Paul as one of the highlights of his professional career.

The thing I liked best about the whole situation was that from the beginning to the end the relationship between the members of the orchestra and myself was one of a really special friendship. Completely a first-name operation ... I respected them and liked them, and it was the kind of relationship that I've never really found again. I think in a way it spoiled me for the later realities of professional conducting ... It was easy music playing. It was a good atmosphere and I think the musicians enjoyed it. They felt comfortable and secure, and they felt cared for. And we put on very, very good concerts.

Review

Copland: *Appalachian Spring, Suite*; Ives: *Three Places in New England*; The Saint Paul Chamber Orchestra, Dennis Russell Davies conducting.

A new coupling of Aaron Copland's *Appalachian Spring* and Charles Ives' *Three Places in New England* might not seem to be the most *necessary* release right now, but the recording of the St. Paul Chamber Orchestra from Sound 80 in Minneapolis, mastered using the 3M digital recording system, is a real zinger!

The Copland music is done with its original instrumentation, for thirteen players, but it is the concert suite rather than the complete ballet score ... The Ives triptych is done in the chamber version the composer prepared in 1930 for Nicolas Slonimsky's ensemble, which took the piece on tour to astonished audiences in Los Angeles, Havana, and Paris.

Appalachian Spring comes off here as wonderfully lean and lithe, although some of the solo instruments, the flute especially, sound a bit larger than life. It is the Ives *Three Places* that is the real prize, not only because of conductor Dennis Russell Davies' intensely poetic and rhythmically vital interpretation, but even more by virtue of the textural details that are brought out by the superbly clean recording, which was done in acoustic surroundings ideal for music. The middle "Putnam's Camp" episode is the most spectacular-sounding, but the finale, "The

Housatonic at Stockbridge," achieves a special ecstatic poignancy. Davies' pulse is sure and steady for the opening "Black March," as Ives sometimes called the movement known as "Boston Common."

—*Stereo Review*, May 1979

Chapter Three
All That Glitters

The stream of people that flowed into Minneapolis'
Orchestra Hall for the opening concert of The Saint Paul
Chamber Orchestra's 1983-1984 season was not a typical
SPCO audience. For one thing, it was a heavily Minneapolis
crowd—just as the managers at the SPCO had hoped it
would be. (This was the third year in a row that the orchestra
had opened its season in Minneapolis, hoping to expand its
fan base.) But it also was an audience consisting of a larger
than usual number of classical music neophytes, which,
again, was understandable. Many of them had come not to
hear The Saint Paul Chamber Orchestra so much as to bask
in the starlight of the evening's three announced soloists:
the SPCO's fiddle-playing conductor, Pinchas Zukerman;
Zukerman's close friend and mentor, Isaac Stern; and the
eleven-year-old violin sensation, Midori Goto.

Pinchas Zukerman and Isaac Stern share a
special moment with eleven-year-old guest
soloist, Midori Goto, following the SPCO
performance on September 12, 1983.

Left: National publications frequently ran
this publicity photo with articles trumpeting
Pinchas Zukerman's arrival in Saint Paul.

The night was billed as "Generations of Music." Zukerman was widely considered
a protégé of Stern's. Midori was a former student of Zukerman's and had come to the
maestro's attention two years earlier at the Aspen Music Festival. Zukerman, upon
hearing her play for the first time, declared that he had "just witnessed a miracle." The
hype surrounding Midori was considerable and the 2,500 or so people who had flocked
to Orchestra Hall were eager to be enchanted. They were not disappointed.

Midori wowed the audience with what *Saint Paul Pioneer Press* music critic Roy
Close described as a "dazzling performance" of the finale of the Saint-Saens Violin
Concerto No. 3. Then, just before intermission, she joined Zukerman and Stern in
a "lively, appealing presentation" of the opening movement of the Vivaldi Concerto
for Three Violins in F Major. The pre-teen prodigy with the three-quarter-size violin
easily upstaged her more experienced colleagues. Indeed, Close judged her intonation
"probably the most accurate of the trio's." Zukerman, Stern, and the orchestra seemed
delighted to play second fiddle, so to speak, to such a charming and gifted young
musician. Hardly anyone on stage or in the audience could keep from smiling.

The second half of the program began with an extended tribute to Stern, who was
honored for his "forty-year commitment to bringing music to Minnesota." A quintet
of dignitaries—Zukerman, Minneapolis Mayor Don Fraser, Saint Paul Mayor George
Latimer, outgoing SPCO Board Chairman John Myers, and former Governor Elmer
L. Andersen—all heaped praise on the honored guest soloist. Stern, who had become
something of a regular visitor to the Twin Cities, was visibly moved.

The rest of the concert was a mixture of Mozart (the Sinfonia Concertante in E-flat
with Stern on violin and Zukerman on viola) and Mendelssohn (with Stern soloing
on the Violin Concerto in E-minor). *Minneapolis Star and Tribune* reviewer Michael

Anthony—Zukerman's most relentless critic—peppered his praise of Stern's playing with a cutting description of the conductor's double-duty musicianship. "Zukerman played the viola and made occasional conducting gestures with his bow," he wrote, "as though hailing a taxi." The audience, less familiar than most SPCO crowds in concert-going etiquette, greeted the end of each movement with enthusiastic applause. Anthony, mortified by the audience's behavior, laid much of the blame on Zukerman. "His vocabulary of conductor's body language is not large enough yet to control such outbursts," he concluded.

Roy Close of the *Pioneer Press* was more forgiving. "Music and good feelings were dispensed in approximately equal proportions," he wrote. Midori performed "with the skill—and confidence—of a mature artist." Zukerman "was beside himself with delight." Stern played "with the warm feeling of a man donning a pair of comfortable old gloves."

Close ended his review with the briefest of codas. "The orchestra," he wrote, "played well all evening."

Instant Cachet

The $1.25 million fund drive that breathed new financial life into the SPCO during its 1978-1979 season probably never would have succeeded had the orchestra's board not made the savvy decision to hire Pinchas Zukerman as its new music director. Zukerman

was a bona fide international star—a supremely talented violinist (and violist) who could coax sounds from his fiddle that made audiences gasp. The fact that a musician of his caliber had agreed to become the next conductor of the SPCO provided powerful evidence that the orchestra was indeed a world-class institution worthy of considerable financial support. Zukerman's name gave the SPCO an instant cachet it had never had before, and it made the $1.25 million fundraising goal almost ridiculously easy to meet.

Over the years, the story of how Zukerman ended up in Saint Paul has become somewhat muddled, but the broad outline is clear. In November 1978, while Dennis Russell Davies was on sabbatical and the SPCO board was confronting its latest financial crisis, Zukerman and his

Zukerman had established himself as one of the world's top violinists by the time he signed on as the SPCO's new music director in 1980.

wife, flutist Eugenia Zukerman, performed in a series of concerts with the SPCO. It was Zukerman's second appearance with the orchestra, but his first as violinist *and* conductor. At some point during his stay in the Twin Cities—probably during a discussion with Richard Johnson, the husband of the orchestra board's former vice-president, Dolores Johnson—the subject of Davies's resignation came up. Zukerman indicated that the SPCO job intrigued him and word of his interest quickly made its way to Preston

Townley, the chairman of the search committee. Townley set up a committee meeting to find out just how serious Zukerman might be about coming to Saint Paul. "As soon as I knew he was interested," Townley later recalled, "I knew that he was the one I wanted."

Zukerman was interested in the job, but there was a catch: He would accept the position only if the orchestra added eight new players. Twenty-six was too small for his liking. He knew that the addition of eight musicians would cost a lot of money the financially strapped orchestra did not currently have, but he was adamant. "Raise the money," he told the committee, "and we'll talk."

With Zukerman's name now dangling as an incentive and the board of directors reenergized by its new president, John Myers, fundraising proceeded quickly. "It was amazing how fast it all happened," Zukerman said. "Within a month, two months, they had raised the money and were back on the phone to me."

Although he wouldn't formally sign his contract until much later, Zukerman spent much of the following year planning his debut as the SPCO's new music director. By early 1980, he was ready. At a well-attended presentation at the Saint Paul Athletic Club, Zukerman announced his plans for the upcoming season. He told the roomful of board members, musicians, and reporters that the orchestra's main subscription series, the Capital Series, would now offer two performances of each program, effectively doubling in size. The Baroque Series would consist of eight programs instead of six. The Perspectives Series—the showcase for New Music—would continue under the direction of the orchestra's new "special consultant for contemporary programs," composer-pianist Marc Neikrug. The season also would feature an impressive lineup of guest artists including Isaac Stern, pianist Daniel Barenboim, cellist Leonard Rose, and harpsichordist Ralph Kirkpatrick. Zukerman, clearly relishing the moment, called his decision to join the SPCO "the most important musical step I've taken in the past twelve years."

Over the next few months, more details of Zukerman's arrangement with the SPCO began to filter out. The orchestra would, as he had demanded, add eight new players—five for the 1980-1981 season and three more during the final two years of his contract. He would conduct the orchestra ten weeks in the Twin Cities and two weeks on the road. His salary would begin at around $120,000 a year and go up from there. Some critics fretted that the orchestra would never be able to absorb the additional costs associated with Zukerman's six-digit salary, eight extra musicians, big-name soloists, and significantly expanded performance schedule, but Zukerman expressed confidence that it would all work out. "We have to put 50 percent more people in the audience," he said.

Fiddler on the Podium

Many of the audience members who packed the O'Shaughnessy Auditorium for the opening concert of the SPCO's 1980-1981 season were prepared to be dazzled. Others came as skeptics. Ever since the news broke that Pinchas Zukerman would take the podium in Saint Paul, much of the music world had buzzed with speculation. Would Zukerman, an accomplished soloist with limited experience as a conductor, know what to do with a baton in his hand? Like others in the audience, the reviewer for *High Fidelity* magazine did his best to keep an open mind.

Though the metaphor did spring to mind, Zukerman-at-the-podium was not an instance of Samuel Johnson's dog walking on its hind legs—the point being, as Dr. Johnson saw it, that one ought not to ask how well the dog did it, but simply to relish the fact that he could do it at all. Zukerman, after all, is no longer a novice conductor. He has stood on his hind legs and conducted a number of the nation's major orchestras in recent seasons, and for the past two summers has served as music director of London's South Bank Festival.

Some critics were skeptical of the new SPCO music director's conducting ability. Donal Henehan of the *New York Times* wrote that Zukerman was "more clearly a great musician ... than a great conductor."

Even before the music began, concertgoers could tell that things had changed. The programs they held in their hands were printed on heavy, flat-finished paper with an elegant typeface. The musicians took their seats onstage dressed not in ascots and blue velvet, but white ties and black tails. From backstage wafted an unearthly sound—gorgeous, soaring arpeggios that could only have been produced by the man nearly everyone in the audience had come to see and hear. Finally, the new conductor walked onstage to exuberant applause and took his place on the podium.

It was an evening of Mozart—just Mozart—and in that respect it was a preview of everything that was to come that season. Fully half of the pieces programmed for the revamped Capital Series were Mozart compositions. The evening began with Zukerman on the podium, guiding the orchestra through the Adagio and Fugue in C Minor. Then the podium was removed and Zukerman returned to the stage with his violin—a Guarneri—in hand. He took his place in the orchestra's arc and launched into the Concerto No. 5 in A Major, his bow coaxing music from both his violin and his orchestra. After intermission came what many considered the highlight of the evening: Zukerman's inspired interpretation of the *Jupiter* symphony. It was, wrote *Saint Paul Pioneer Press* critic David Hawley, "a fine demonstration of conducting skill and acumen, a sensitive and significant performance."

When it was all over, the audience rose to its feet and repeatedly summoned back Zukerman for curtain calls. The mood in the hall was ecstatic. The fiddler had proved he could waggle a baton without embarrassing himself. The orchestra, with five new string players, had produced a thicker, lusher sound than it had ever made for Dennis Russell Davies. "In all, Zukerman gave his audience cause to look forward to more of his Mozart," freelance music critic D.R. Martin concluded. "And there will be plenty of that."

As the season progressed, Zukerman continued to enchant audiences with his music making and with what *Newsweek* called his "engaging mixture of boyish exuberance, streetwise swagger and a certain shyness." The people of Saint Paul had rarely witnessed such star power so close up and they were savoring the experience. The box office tally at the end of the season showed the results: a 71 percent jump in ticket revenue over the previous year.

By most accounts, the players in the orchestra were nearly as smitten with Zukerman as the audiences were. "The musicians seem to enjoy working with him," the *Minneapolis Tribune's* Michael Anthony wrote. "A few have spoken in near-rapturous tones about the initial performances and rehearsals this season." During its first few months with Zukerman at the helm, the orchestra made four recordings for CBS. In February 1981, it made its first tour of South America, a trip that many players considered a true bonding experience. The following May it made the first of several annual appearances at New York's Carnegie Hall. There were definite benefits to having a big-name musician as your conductor, as the players of the SPCO were quickly beginning to comprehend.

Still, questions lingered about Zukerman's ability with the baton. Many of his musicians—trained as they were to follow the precision conducting of Dennis Russell Davies—found Zukerman's technique hard to follow. "We got to the point where he'd give a downbeat and you'd come in when you came in," cellist Eddie Blitz recalled. "It was always a delayed beat." Music critics, including Donal Henehan of the *New York Times*, noted Zukerman's deficiencies on the podium and wondered whether he would ever become a first-rate maestro.

The orchestra shares a laugh with Concertmaster Romuald Tecco and Music Director Pinchas Zukerman. Zukerman's first season with the SPCO was a hit with audiences and musicians alike.

> *Still only a few years old as a conductor, Zukerman has some distance to travel before mastering his alternate craft. His beat can be unpredictable and mushy. Sometimes his cues and other gestures seem more related to his sympathetic reaction to the music than to any specific instrumental or ensemble purpose. He seems to be more intent on encouraging his orchestra to play with nuance, phrase and subtle tone than in enforcing precision, martinet style. He is, in short, more clearly a great musician at this point than a great conductor.*

Zukerman's programming also provided an easy target. His reliance on Mozart and other crowd-pleasing, Old-World composers struck critics as unnecessarily conservative. Even Zukerman admitted that he could have done better. "I think it was the worst season

I've seen anybody have," he said in a self-critique of his first year.

Many critics were especially bothered by Zukerman's approach to New Music. Although he had brought in his friend, Marc Neikrug, to oversee the orchestra's modern repertoire, he purged New Music from the popular Capital Series. In a letter to a disappointed season ticket-holder, the SPCO's new managing director, David Richardson, explained that the orchestra had little choice but to remove contemporary music from its main programs. "We are trying to enlarge our audience considerably," he wrote. "If the traditional balance for this Orchestra has been upset to your displeasure, then I am sorry." For an orchestra that had earned a reputation for adventurous programming under Dennis Russell Davies, the disappearance of twentieth century music from the Capital Series during Zukerman's first season was hard to ignore. The National Endowment for the Arts, noting the SPCO's "seeming decline of contemporary music programming," responded by cutting off all new music funding to the orchestra.

Nevertheless, as the 1980-1981 season came to a close, it seemed premature to say Zukerman's honeymoon with the SPCO was over. His admirers looked forward to hearing more of his orchestra's sumptuous music making. Critics of his conducting skills seemed willing to give him more time. Even his musicians were eager to see what he would do next. "The feeling is that we have a coup with Pinky," said Tom Kornacker, the orchestra's new principal second violin and one of Zukerman's former Juilliard classmates. "He came here and generated the kind of enthusiasm that has not been seen here ever before."

The Price of Success

The next two years under Zukerman were among the most successful the SPCO had ever experienced. The orchestra toured extensively throughout the United States and booked running engagements at Carnegie Hall, the Kennedy Center in Washington, D.C., and the Ravinia Festival in Chicago. It recorded a series of acclaimed recordings with RCA and CBS. It made regular appearances on Minnesota Public Radio's nationally distributed program, *Saint Paul Sunday Morning*. The number of subscribers continued to increase. The concert season expanded. The SPCO was becoming one of the hottest tickets in town. Advertisers, including the Dayton's department store chain (which featured Zukerman and the orchestra in a Christmas catalog), began looking at the SPCO in a new light. Generating publicity had never been easier. "There was no need to sell the orchestra during those first years of Zukerman," the new artistic administrator, Sarah Solotaroff explained. "Everything came to us. Everybody wanted to do something with The Saint Paul Chamber Orchestra with him as the head of it."

It didn't hurt that Zukerman reinvented himself in a few visible respects during the run-up to his second season. The conductor who took the stage at Orchestra Hall on September 24, 1981, was a sleeker version of his former self—forty pounds lighter and clean-shaven. Critics twittered about his "trim and handsome new look" and speculated about the effect his lost weight might have on the orchestra's sound. "Instead of the [overly] caloric tendencies of many of last year's performances, we have more of a *nouvelle cuisine* chamber orchestra playing under Zukerman this fall," freelance reviewer D.R. Martin wrote. "Things sound leaner, more responsive, more exciting."

Zukerman suddenly seemed more comfortable with a baton than he had during his first season. *Saint Paul Pioneer Press* critic Roy Close noted that Zukerman was now employing his "formerly useless left hand" to cue entrances and control dynamics. "In short," Close wrote, "he is beginning to be at home on the podium."

As Zukerman settled in, the financial turn-around that had begun the year before accelerated. Earned income (revenues from ticket sales, recording contracts, tour dates, and the like) almost doubled during his second season with the orchestra. Corporate donations rose more than 30 percent. In March 1982, the SPCO board rewarded him with a raise and a contract extension through the 1985-1986 season. "Many good things have happened to The Saint Paul Chamber Orchestra since September 1980," managing director David Richardson said, "and the major factor in making them all possible is Pinchas Zukerman." A major factor, certainly, but not the only one.

Some listeners believed Zukerman's new slim, clean-shaven look matched the orchestra's "leaner, more responsive" sound.

In the three years since assuming the chairmanship of the SPCO's board of directors, John Myers had transformed the orchestra's leadership structure. He expanded the board from thirty-four to seventy members and recruited heavily from the corporate sector. He also instituted a host of "thou shalts": Board members were expected to faithfully attend board meetings, actively raise funds for the orchestra, and contribute significant sums from their own pockets. He had, in essence, professionalized the board and, in the process, impressed the orchestra's music director. "John set out to improve things," Zukerman explained. "He brought new people on the board— people who understood that non-profit organizations weren't there to make money, but to lose money intelligently and correctly. Believe me, that's something that a lot of businessmen don't get."

The two men became, in Zukerman's words, "inseparable." Myers admired Zukerman's tenacious drive to make the SPCO an internationally renowned ensemble. Zukerman respected Myers's keen business instincts. They quickly forged an alliance that helped Zukerman begin shaping the orchestra into the image he envisioned.

About a month after Zukerman signed his contract extension, the SPCO's managing director David Richardson resigned amid "reports of dissatisfaction with his leadership." Zukerman had never warmed to Richardson and the resignation had all the markings of a palace coup. A few weeks later, the board of directors chose Dick Contee, the former

Although community outreach received less emphasis after Zukerman's arrival, SPCO musicians like Carolyn Daws continued to work with local music students.

Above: In March 1982, Zukerman announced he had signed a new three-year contract that would keep him with the SPCO through the 1985-1986 season. Joining him at the news conference were SPCO Managing Director David Richardson and Board Chairman John Myers. Richardson resigned about a month later and was replaced by Dick Contee.

director of the Dayton Hudson Foundation, to replace Richardson. Contee knew little about music or orchestras, but he did know how to raise money locally—a talent Zukerman prized. Zukerman had—with John Myers's blessing—taken it upon himself to recruit Contee and, as the story went, had found it necessary to convince Contee that he was the right man for the job. When Contee demurred, claiming he couldn't even hum Brahms's lullaby, Zukerman responded, "That's okay—I can."

Contee's fundraising abilities were important because the SPCO was becoming an increasingly expensive operation to run. The orchestra was, in some ways, choking on its own success. "The budget went up very rapidly," Sarah Solotaroff explained. "We were making tons of money, but then we were spending tons of money."

As Contee soon discovered, the SPCO was—despite its recent success—in big financial trouble. "We're looking at cutbacks," he told a reporter. "We'll make adjustments to stay in the black, but it hurts, there's no question."

By the end of the 1982-1983 season, the extent of those adjustments had become clear. The orchestra faced a $200,000 deficit and everyone in the organization was pitching in to help make up the shortfall. Zukerman took a $14,000 pay cut. The musicians agreed to perform one concert without compensation, effectively reducing their salaries by 2.5 percent. The administrative staff gave up two days' salary and one month's contribution to their pension fund. Board members pledged to contribute $30,000 of their own money and to raise an additional $30,000 from friends and colleagues.

During the bulk of his first three seasons, Zukerman had managed to avoid the pain of budget cuts, but the price of success was beginning to catch up with him and the orchestra. Big-name soloists were expensive. Expanded concert schedules were expensive. Additional musicians were expensive. Zukerman himself, with his six-figure salary, was expensive. The austerity measures Contee had just put in place ensured that the orchestra would open the 1983-1984 season in sound financial condition, but there was no assurance that it would stay that way. Budgets would have to remain tight at the SPCO, and that was unfortunate because Zukerman had some big ideas he was determined to bring to fruition.

The Ordway Music Theatre under construction, 1984.

Home

The Saint Paul Chamber Orchestra had always been something of a transient group, shuttling from one venue to another. The Arts and Science Center and the O'Shaughnessy Auditorium had both served as primary performance spaces over the years, but neither qualified as a true home. There was a growing sense that the SPCO needed to settle down.

Almost from the moment he arrived in Saint Paul, Pinchas Zukerman had been on the lookout for a new home for his orchestra. In 1980, he visited the old Union Depot train station in the city's Lowertown neighborhood to determine whether it would make a good auditorium. With cellist Peter Howard playing his instrument at one end of the cavernous space, Zukerman sampled the building's acoustics. "It was perfect," he later recalled. "The sound just dissipated perfectly." The depot, which had sent off its last train nearly a decade earlier, would have made an impressive home for the SPCO, but plans for the proposed conversion never got very far. Another idea was in the works, and it soon caught Zukerman's fancy.

Sally Irvine, the granddaughter of Lucius Pond Ordway, one of the founders of the 3M Company, had recently concluded that Saint Paul needed a new performance space—she was peeved that there was so little to do in downtown after dark—and had retained an architect to work up a preliminary design for a site across the street from Rice Park. When Zukerman heard about Irvine's plans, he decided to find out whether her proposed performance venue might accommodate his orchestra. He paid her a visit at her "nice little house" on Summit Avenue. They immediately hit it off.

> *She looked at me and said, "You must be Pinky Zukerman. What kind of name is Pinky?" So I told her the story. She said, "Do you want some cake?" I said no. "She said, "Well, have some cake." … I loved her. I just loved her. We talked about everything except the [concert hall]. She asked me where I was born and we talked about my parents and Auschwitz and the Nazis. Really a wonderful woman.*

The conductor and the cake-pushing heiress developed a fast rapport and their first meeting led to others. Eventually the conversation turned to her concert hall plans. When Zukerman finally saw the prototype, he was dismayed. The design called for a small theater-in-the-round with room for just seven hundred seats. He urged Irvine to reconsider—to think bigger and less round. To his relief, she listened. "I've got to hand it to her," he said. "She saw right away that the shape was wrong, the acoustics were wrong, the size was uneconomical."

Zukerman inserted himself into the design process and the final results showed his influence. The new Ordway Music Theatre, designed by Benjamin Thompson, would include a large, primary auditorium—a 1,815-seat, horseshoe-shaped performance space reminiscent of the Fenice Opera House in Venice, Italy—and a smaller 315-seat studio theater. It was to be a multipurpose concert hall capable of accommodating the needs of its three main occupants: the SPCO, the Minnesota Opera Company, and the Schubert Club.

As construction progressed, Zukerman and his musicians did everything they could to reinforce the impression that they would be the Ordway's primary tenants. Indeed, first-year projections showed that the SPCO's Ordway bookings equaled the combined total of the Minnesota Opera and the Schubert Club. "Ordway will give us an identification with a specific hall and a specific sound," Zukerman explained. "People will hear 'Ordway' and they will say, 'Oh, The Saint Paul Chamber Orchestra.'" The musicians, too, sought to exert their influence on the final product. In the months leading up to the hall's grand opening, for example, they pressured the Ordway board to install backstage lockers for their private use. Given their assumption that the Ordway was, above all, the new home of the SPCO, it was not surprising that Zukerman and his players expected to be the feature attraction at the hall's grand opening in January 1985.

To their dismay, it was not be. The gala debut of the Ordway Music Theatre showcased a Schubert Club recital by soprano Leontyne Price. The SPCO had to wait until the following night.

Although the Schubert Club performance was, in the words of *Saint Paul Pioneer Press* critic Roy Close, "the more glamorous affair," the SPCO's Ordway debut seemed to create a bigger buzz. "Indeed," Close wrote, "it seemed evident that this was the event many Twin Cities concertgoers had been waiting for. Price's recital had been a grand and splendid occasion, but the chamber orchestra's debut was to be the first real test of the Ordway's acoustics."

The initial reviews were encouraging. *Minneapolis Star and Tribune* critic Michael Anthony described the Ordway's acoustics as "mellow, warm, civilized, [and] unaggressive." Roy Close called the Ordway a "live" hall that made true pianissimos possible—and accentuated Zukerman's distracting habit of stomping his foot for emphasis. The new concert hall was neither a disaster nor an acoustic wonder. But it was a beautiful performance space that would help anchor Saint Paul's late-century revival. And it finally gave The Saint Paul Chamber Orchestra a home.

The SPCO's Ordway debut concert on January 9, 1985, opened with the singing of the "Star Spangled Banner" and a brief choral piece, Mozart's *Regina Coeli*.

But all was not well at the new hall on Rice Park. In the three years between the Ordway's groundbreaking and its opening, construction costs had ballooned from $23 million to $42 million. The Ordway family augmented its original $10 million pledge with an additional $5 million contribution. A $10 million loan from the McKnight Foundation and a $27 million bond-financing package from the Saint Paul Port Authority helped bridge the remaining gap, but the cost overruns left the Ordway board little room to maneuver once construction was complete. Financial problems would eventually force the Ordway board to make moneymaking scheduling decisions that strained its relations with the SPCO.

The orchestra was having problems of its own. The 1983-1984 season had ended with a $150,000 deficit. Bill Contee publicly downplayed the news, pointing out that excitement about the Ordway had sparked a 19 percent jump in subscription sales, but financial worries persisted. In the weeks before the Ordway's grand opening, the musicians, who played the first half of the season without a contract, threatened to go on strike. A last-minute compromise averted a potentially ugly and embarrassing work stoppage, but the acrimonious negotiations had poisoned relations between the players and management. Tensions were growing within the SPCO—and Pinchas Zukerman was growing restless.

Sour Notes

In May 1985, at the conclusion of the Ordway debut season, the SPCO board announced that it had voted to extend Pinchas Zukerman's contract. Zukerman was committed to the orchestra only through the 1986-1987 season. The extension would ensure that he stayed with the SPCO through June 1990. The news release announcing the vote stated that Zukerman was expected to sign the new contract "within the next few weeks," but Zukerman never signed.

Relations between the SPCO's music director and the board had been tense for some time. The two parties had begun talking about a new contract more than a year earlier, and Zukerman had made it clear that he intended to drive a hard bargain. Although he wanted a raise and more time off, his main demands concerned the orchestra's identity and its long-term survival: He wanted more musicians and he wanted the board to create an endowment.

Ever since his arrival in Saint Paul, Zukerman had been fighting off rumors that he planned to expand the SPCO until it was virtually indistinguishable from the much larger Minnesota Orchestra. He had fed such suspicions with his initial demand to add eight musicians. By his second season with the orchestra, he was forced to confront the rumors head on. "We're not going to do Bruckner or Mahler," he insisted. "Sometimes it will be necessary, for better programming, to enlarge the orchestra, but the additional musicians will not be under contract."

Although Zukerman did not add Bruckner or Mahler to the SPCO's repertoire, he did add Beethoven, and Beethoven required extra players, which Zukerman hired on a freelance basis. Sophisticated concertgoers noticed the change, and some, including Marion Fake of Saint Paul, wrote to express their displeasure.

In the fall of 1985, The Saint Paul Chamber Orchestra and the Minnesota Opera collaborated with the Ordway Music Theatre to present the American premiere of Oliver Knussen's *Where the Wild Things Are*, a 45-minute fantasy opera based on Maurice Sendak's popular children's book.

> *After finding Beethoven's Second Symphony on last Sunday's program ... I am aware of an uneasy feeling about the direction of the orchestra ...*
>
> *The orchestra itself is certainly larger than four years ago. But it seems clear now that an enlarged orchestra means a large orchestra repertoire. We appear to be moving toward a St. Paul version of the Minnesota Orchestra.*
>
> *People of St. Paul have indicated by their support over ten years that they want a chamber orchestra—small, delicate—with plenty of opportunity to hear excellent individual instrumentalists in the orchestra. We do not want the old warhorses, but an investigation of the vast chamber orchestra repertoire that is unique, musical and varied.*

During the latter part of his tenure, Zukerman regularly expressed his desire to expand the orchestra beyond its current complement of thirty-four players.

Zukerman continued to insist he had no desire to turn the SPCO into a symphony orchestra, but during his third season in Saint Paul, he went before the SPCO board and formally asked for more string players. He didn't say exactly how many he wanted, just that he needed enough to play a broad range of music written between 1600 and the present—excluding "the large works of the Romantic composers." He even suggested changing the ensemble's name to "The Saint Paul Classical Orchestra," which, he pointed out, would allow the orchestra to continue using the initials SPCO.

Over the next few years, Zukerman continued to lobby unsuccessfully for more musicians. Not even his close relationship with John Myers could overcome the board's reluctance. Part of the problem was that he seemed unable to decide how many extra musicians he really wanted. At one point, he said he wanted an orchestra of forty-three players (nine more than he had). Later he said he needed only thirty-nine. Many board members were unsure of Zukerman's motives and they were reluctant to sign off on an ill-defined expansion plan that would significantly increase costs and could erode the SPCO's distinctive small-orchestra character. It was not surprising that the contract extension the board approved in the spring of 1985 said nothing about additional musicians.

The contract did seek to meet Zukerman's other primary demand—that the board raise a substantial endowment to stabilize the orchestra's perpetually unstable finances. Everyone on the board realized that the orchestra needed an endowment—the SPCO was one of the few major orchestras in the country without one—but they also knew raising the funds for such a nest egg would be a gargantuan task. As an editorial in the *Saint Paul Pioneer Press* pointed out, the SPCO was not the only worthy local organization looking for financial help.

> *The orchestra's needs must be weighed against others in the community and against the community's giving capacity. Aside from ongoing solicitations for the arts, the Ordway Music Theater board is trying to raise an endowment of $5 million and finish paying off construction costs. With cutbacks in government support for the arts and in human services, private givers are being besieged for more contributions.*

Although the 1985 contract extension did not specifically provide for the creation of an endowment, it did confirm that the board would hire a consulting firm to develop a program for an endowment fund drive. The board hoped that the contract's endowment provision would be enough to convince Zukerman to sign on for another three years, but the music director was not impressed. Zukerman's close friend John Myers had died in June 1984, leaving him without an effective advocate on the board. When a reporter asked him what he would do if the endowment campaign failed to materialize, his answer was blunt. "Then I must think twice about continuing with the orchestra," he said. "People have always said that I think way too big. Maybe I do. In that case I have to rethink what my obligations are in terms of this orchestra, and what's best for them."

Zukerman was becoming brasher in his dealings with the board and more unpredictable in his behavior with the orchestra and the public. Some players complained about a tense atmosphere during rehearsals, "It was bad," one of the musicians recalled. "You didn't even want to go to work ... You got a knot in your stomach and you wondered what you were going to have to endure." Concertgoers, too, began noticing a difference in the normally charming conductor. During a tour of Southern states, Zukerman showed up late for a concert in Lafayette, Louisiana, then proceeded to offend much of the audience. "Mr. Zukerman was very angry toward the orchestra and toward the audience," one concertgoer wrote in a complaint to the SPCO board of directors. "We were sorely insulted and disappointed."

In early January 1986, nearly eight months after the SPCO board approved his never-to-be-signed contract extension, Pinchas Zukerman announced his resignation. He would stay on, he said, until the end of the 1986-1987 season, as stipulated in his current contract. (He had earlier signed a one-year extension.) In his announcement, Zukerman confessed that being a music director was "not in my blood," and expressed a desire to return to playing violin full time. Although he did not dwell on his efforts to expand the orchestra or secure an endowment, he made it clear he had wearied of his financial battles with the board. "I can no longer sit around and wait for promises, however sincere they may be," he said. "When I [ask for] something, I expect to have it in six months, not six years."

In the months that followed, Zukerman occasionally vented his frustrations in ways that failed to endear him to board members or the people of Saint Paul. He meddled in the board's efforts to find a replacement for Dick Contee, who had left the orchestra at the beginning of the year. At a board meeting in April he warned that "if we are known as an institution which doesn't allow its music director to enlarge the orchestra, then we will have no credibility." He told a reporter from the *Chicago Sun-Times* that "any board and any musicians who get to the point that they think they can control and run the organization better than Pinky Zukerman are musically illiterate." In an interview with Gene Shalit on NBC television's *The Today Show*, he complained that the SPCO board had failed to "meet me halfway" on "all kinds of things." His comments received widespread publicity and prompted a caustic response from *St. Paul Pioneer Press and Dispatch* columnist Nick Coleman.

> *My, my, Pinky is peeved. Let's see what he means when he says St. Paul wouldn't meet him halfway. Let's see just how shabbily Mr. Z. has been treated by this little backwater burg.*
>
> *First, we should note that Pinky is paid $300,000 a year for 19 weeks of work. That kind of money would buy a lot of oboe players, and it seems like a lot of do-re-mi for a job that doesn't require heavy lifting. It's also five times what Pinky's predecessor, Dennis Russell Davies, was paid.*
>
> *Let's also remember that the orchestra took a chance when it hired Pinky despite his lack of experience as a conductor and music director. And let's remember that St. Paul went to bat for Pinky. When he said St. Paul needed a new music hall, St. Paul dug deep and the $46 million Ordway came to pass. When Pinky raised his pinky, St. Paul usually came a-running.*

Not everyone was as eager as Coleman to be rid of the SPCO's mercurial music director. Zukerman still had one season left with the orchestra and now that he had given up fighting with the board, many SPCO fans hoped he would devote all his efforts to making music. "Area music lovers have held Mr. Zukerman in sturdy affection for too long to let his remarks do more than briefly rankle," one of Coleman's editorial page colleagues on the *Pioneer Press and Dispatch* wrote. "May he take the musicians that he has and continue to make sweet sounds and beautiful music in this, his final year with them."

"My Last Farewell"

For those who remembered Zukerman's all-Mozart debut with the orchestra six years earlier, the program he put together for the first concert of his final season in Saint Paul must have come as something of a shock. He devoted the entire evening to twentieth century music: Richard Strauss's Symphony for Winds in E-Flat, selections from George Gershwin's *Porgy and Bess*, and the premiere of *Remembering Child (Samantha Smith in memory)* by Danish composer Per Nørgård. Even Michael Anthony, the *Minneapolis Star Tribune* critic who had been so hard on Zukerman in the past, was impressed. "If nothing else," he wrote, "the program Zukerman selected made a strong case for the stylistic diversity of the music of the past half-century."

Saint Paul Mayor George Latimer greets Pinchas Zukerman onstage before Zukerman's final Friday performance as the SPCO's music director.

Criticism of Zukerman's perceived bias against contemporary music had persisted throughout his tenure in Saint Paul, but much of that criticism was unfair and ill informed. Although the orchestra under Zukerman had once tended to "ghetto-ize" (a term commonly used by Sarah Solotaroff and other SPCO insiders) New Music into the Perspectives Series, it had gradually changed its approach over the years. As Michael Anthony noted, "odd, interesting works began to appear on the programs as well as new and recent pieces." Indeed, a 1986 survey of SPCO programming found that the orchestra had performed or scheduled thirty-three world premieres since Zukerman arrived—three more than it had presented during Dennis Russell Davies's tenure.

As the 1986-1987 season progressed, it seemed evident that Zukerman was weaning himself from the SPCO. Of the orchestra's sixteen Ordway concerts, he conducted just five. Despite the rancor of the previous few years, he intended to bow out as gracefully as possible.

Zukerman's farewell performance on the afternoon of May 24, 1987, was a fitting send-off. There was the requisite contingent of "Pinky's friends" (Isaac Stern and pianist Misha Dichter). There was Bach (Concerto for Two Violins), there was Handel (*Dixit Dominus* with the Minnesota Chorale), and there was Beethoven (Symphony No. 2). Dignitaries, including Saint Paul Mayor George Latimer and Lieutenant Governor Marlene Johnson, showered praise on the outgoing music director. Zukerman kept his thank-yous short, borrowing a line from another well-known—and considerably less talented—violinist. "Call this my last farewell," he said, quoting the comedian Jack Benny. "I'll see you as I have many times—with a violin under my chin."

Pinchas Zukerman's seven years in Saint Paul had been, in the words of critic Michael Anthony, "baffling, enlightening, amusing, discouraging, enlivening, perplexing and daunting," and above all, "never dull." During his watch, the orchestra had tripled its subscription base, significantly expanded its concert season, and raised its international stature through recordings, tours, and associations with some of the world's greatest musicians. Zukerman had helped make it possible for the SPCO to move into its first true home, the Ordway. He had enlarged the orchestra and changed its sound. He had mesmerized audiences with his playing and confounded them with his conducting. His was an impressive legacy fraught with contradictions, and his musicians—some of whom felt they had been relegated to playing in "Pinky's backup band"—had mixed feelings about their departing leader.

"Pinky manages to bring out both the best and the worst in the orchestra at different times," principal hornist Herb Winslow said. "Sometimes he gets a natural flow going and everything works beautifully. Other times the concept he has in mind just doesn't get across to the musicians because it is just so hard for him to explain what he is looking for."

"He didn't seem to grow as a conductor," violist Evelina Chao added. "That frustrated me because I saw he had such great talent. He never wielded the baton with the same confidence, the same expertise, he did with his violin and bow. Maybe that was too much to expect."

On the Tuesday before his final concert with the SPCO, Zukerman guided the orchestra through a pair of rehearsals. The last piece he played with his musicians was a composition by Antonin Dvořák, the Romance in F Minor for Violin and Orchestra. After the rehearsal, the orchestra's principal bassist, Christopher Brown, wrote down his impressions.

Pinchas Zukerman at play.

These moments I will never forget. Pinky turned toward the orchestra and simply poured out his heart with his playing. It was gracious, it was unselfish, it was truly beyond words. Pinky outdid himself with each phrase, playing his violin open and clearly, speaking to us with everything he had.

To me, he was saying "thank you" to us, his orchestra, on his terms: with music, not with words or batons. As I was playing, I was so moved I felt embarrassed for allowing myself to get carried away. I was thinking things like: how no conductor can be as intimate with our orchestra as Pinky can be when playing his violin with us; how no one—no one—can play that piece like Pinky can; how this orchestra does respect Pinky and he respects us.

What Pinky gave us Tuesday was, in my opinion, a private "thank you" given in a most respectful and beautiful way. I am sure I wasn't the only member saying "thank you" to Pinky with every new phrase …

Thank you for this past Tuesday, Pinky. Thank you for the last seven years.

Pinchas Zukerman
Music Director, 1980-1987

No matter how hard he worked at it—and even his harshest critics acknowledged that he worked very hard—Pinchas Zukerman never seemed fully comfortable on the podium. After sitting in on a rehearsal during Zukerman's second season with the SPCO, reporter Susan Perry of *Twin Cities* magazine crafted a vivid description of her subject's conducting style.

Zukerman conducts without the "barrier" of a score. His movements are minimal. Often, he stands like a rooted tree, his feet together, swaying from the waist. He holds his hands high, but keeps his elbows pointed to the ground. That way he avoids straining his right arm, his bowing arm.

Although Zukerman could seem stilted when he stood on a podium, his reserved manner melted away when he stepped down, tucked a violin under his chin, and replaced his baton with a bow. Zukerman believed that good conductors employed "body English" to coax sound from orchestras, and his body seemed to communicate best when he was playing along with his musicians. "You saw the bow arm, you saw the style, and you were able to relate to what he was doing," cellist Eddie Blitz recalled. "He was still the leader, but he was not doing it with a baton. He was doing it with the fiddle."

Whatever his weaknesses as a conductor, Pinchas Zukerman was a magician with the fiddle. Born in Tel Aviv in 1948, Zukerman started playing the violin when he was seven years old. His prodigious talent soon became evident and at the age of twelve, he received an invitation to play for a delegation of visiting musicians, including violinist Isaac Stern and cellist Pablo Casals. "In walked this self-confident gamin," Stern later recalled. "He put his feet down, spread his legs wide, took a stand like a linebacker, stuck out his chin, raised his violin and dared us not to like him." Like him they did. Stern and Casals were so impressed that they helped arrange scholarships to send Zukerman to New York City and Juilliard.

Separated from his family, speaking little English, and thrown into a big city full of temptations, Zukerman rebelled. He skipped classes, refused to practice, smoked cigarettes, and frequented pool halls. He might never have set himself straight had Stern, who had by then assumed the role of surrogate father, not intervened. "He actually opened my ears to make me really listen to myself," Zukerman said.

In 1967, after five years at Juilliard, Zukerman placed first at the prestigious Leventritt International Competition. From there, his career took off. In the decade that followed, Zukerman established himself as one of the finest musicians of his generation. He made records, toured the world, and mastered a second instrument—the viola. The *Times of London* called him a violinist "without peer." *Gramophone* proclaimed that he was "probably the best living viola player." At the age of thirty, Zukerman was at the top of his profession. But it wasn't enough. "I felt what I was doing wasn't getting me anywhere," he explained. I was happy in my musical output, but not in the eventual where-is-it-going-to-go, what-is-it-going-to-be sense."

Zukerman began guest conducting—first at the English Chamber Orchestra in London, and then at others: the New York Philharmonic, the Philadelphia Orchestra, the Los Angeles Philharmonic, the San Francisco Symphony, the Toronto Symphony, the Israel Philharmonic, and the Israel Chamber Orchestra. By the time the opportunity with The Saint Paul Chamber Orchestra presented itself, Zukerman was more than ready to give up the life of an itinerant virtuoso.

But, as Zukerman's seven-year run with the SPCO demonstrated, playing and conducting are two very different things. Virtuosos do not necessarily make the best maestros—or the best music directors. Even Zukerman seemed willing to admit as much as the end of his tenure neared. "The music directorship per se is not in my blood," he said. "I think that I am the wrong person for the job. I probably will never be a music director again." In 1998, eleven years after leaving the SPCO, he took over Canada's National Arts Centre Orchestra, a forty-six-member ensemble that conformed to his ideal size requirements.

Review

Mozart: Violin Concertos No. 3 and 5; Pinchas Zukerman, violin, with The Saint Paul Chamber Orchestra, Zukerman conducting.

At times, Pinchas Zukerman's taste for heart-on-the-sleeve emotionalism and sweet-toned schmaltz has led one to think that a law should be passed banning him from playing any music earlier than Bruch or Wieniawski. But then Zukerman confounds expectations with such recordings as his recent version of Vivaldi's "Four Seasons" or this excellent reading of Mozart's two most popular violin concertos.

Less sticky than usual, Zukerman's style still seems a shade too romantic for Mozart. But one is willing to put up with some excess sweetness in return for the passion and commitment with which Zukerman plays here, not to mention his infallible grasp of the structure of these works.

Perhaps it's Zukerman's adoption of the conductor's role that does the trick. But whatever the reason, these are among the finest large-scale performances of the Mozart concertos—bold in outline, technically superb and, in the best sense, full of heart.

—*Chicago Tribune*, January 30, 1983

Chapter Four

A New Course

———

Regular patrons of The Saint Paul Chamber Orchestra knew what to expect at the beginning of a concert. The minutes before the music began were almost always routine in their formality. Musicians would walk onto the brightly lit stage, one by one, and take their seats. Concertmaster Romuald Tecco would make his entrance to polite applause. Oboist Kathryn Greenbank would provide a concert A, and the hall would fill with the sound of tuning strings and woodwinds. Finally, the conductor—usually Hugh Wolff— would enter from offstage, step onto the podium, raise his baton, and bring the orchestra to life. The whole process was predictable.

It didn't take long for many of the concertgoers who had filtered into the Ordway on the evening of February 19, 1993, to notice that something was different. The stage was dark and the musicians were difficult to make out. Regulars in the audience began twittering with anticipation. They had learned over the past few years to expect imaginative programming from Wolff and the young conductor clearly was toying with convention again.

As *Minneapolis Star Tribune* critic Michael Anthony would later describe it, the evening's music began with "little wisps of string passages" drifting out from the darkness. Then a loud chord shattered the tranquility. The lights came up. Violinists Hanley Daws and Leslie Shank stood in front of the rest of the orchestra, playing solo parts, and Wolff was at his accustomed place on the podium. The opening composition was Alfred Schnittke's *Moz-Art à la Haydn,* a dreamlike patchwork of eighteenth-century-style musical snippets. As the piece approached its conclusion, the sound dissipated, the lights dimmed, and the musicians walked offstage, playing as they went.

Having established a lightness-and-darkness theme for the evening, Wolff left the lights on for the next two pieces—Mozart's Piano Concerto No. 22 in E-flat (with soloist Emanuel Ax) and Aaron Jay Kernis's *Musica Celestis* (with Kernis taking a bow from the audience). But Wolff wasn't about to let the concert end without returning to his theme. His choice for the finale, Haydn's Symphony No. 45—better known as the "Farewell" Symphony—gave him and the orchestra a chance to play with the lights one more time. Haydn had written the symphony to include a bit of stage business (at its premiere in 1772, the musicians snuffed out the candles on their music stands during the final adagio), and Wolff was glad to follow at least the spirit of Haydn's original intent. As the piece wound down, the lights faded and—as Michael Anthony later described it—each musician left the stage, acting as though he or she suddenly remembered "an appointment in another part of town." Finally, Wolff made his exit, leaving Tecco and fellow violinist Thomas Kornacker to complete the symphony as the house went black.

Some members of the audience undoubtedly failed to appreciate Wolff's theatrics, but many others—including Michael Anthony—were entranced. "What's wrong with lighting effects?" Anthony asked. "Concert presenters talk all the time these days about

> It didn't take long for many concertgoers...to notice that something was different...the audience began twittering with anticipation.

Left: Hugh Wolff and the SPCO take Europe by storm in the spring of 1993.

changing tired old concert formats. Maybe a different lighting scheme should accompany each work in every concert. Some would grumble that it distracts from the music. Would it? Maybe people would listen harder."

Help

Pinchas Zukerman's final season with the SPCO had been a turbulent one in many respects. Financially, the orchestra had dug itself a deep hole. It entered the 1986-1987 season with an accumulated deficit of nearly half a million dollars—about a quarter of which was directly attributable to the cancellation of a European tour the previous spring. (Fears of international terrorism following the U.S. bombing of Libya and concerns about lingering health threats after the Chernobyl nuclear plant accident had prompted several musicians to refuse to make the trip.) The orchestra had severed its relationship with United Arts—the old Arts Council—in the fall of 1985 and still hadn't figured out how to replace the more than $400,000 it had received each year from the organization. It also put on hold a $10 million endowment campaign that the orchestra's board had approved, in large part to appease Zukerman.

New President and Managing Director Deborah Borda moved quickly to resolve what she called the SPCO's "music director question."

From a leadership standpoint, the SPCO had rarely seemed so rudderless. It entered the season with a lame duck music director (Zukerman), a board chairman-elect who wasn't sure he wanted to be anything more than a placeholder (Dan Pennie), and an acting general manager who suspected she wouldn't be kept on (Sarah Solotaroff). There was little evidence to suggest that the existing leadership team had a clear plan for addressing the many challenges facing the orchestra in the post-Zukerman era. Then help arrived.

Deborah Borda joined the SPCO in September 1986, at about the same time Zukerman was beginning his final season with the orchestra. The board hired her to fill the vacancy left by the departure of Dick Contee nine months earlier, and gave her a new, dual title—president and managing director. Borda came to Saint Paul with impressive credentials. A trained violinist and violist, she had climbed the ranks of music management at the Marlboro Festival in Vermont, the Handel and Haydn Society in Boston, and, finally, the San Francisco Symphony. She was known as a dynamic and decisive administrator in the mold of former SPCO general manager Stephen Sell. In a news release announcing her hiring, the board called her "the ideal candidate to move the SPCO into a new era of solid artistic and financial achievement."

During her first few months on the job, Borda moved quickly to assert control over what she judged to be an orchestra adrift. She prodded the board of directors to approve a new $25 million fundraising campaign (including $10 million for an endowment), made Dan Pennie understand how important his chairmanship was to the orchestra's future ("Dan was a real partner in tough times," she said), and hectored Sarah Solotaroff to resign. She bought more time to search for Zukerman's successor by convincing former Minnesota Orchestra music director Stanislaw Skrowaczewski to take over the orchestra on an interim basis. "There was a sense of restoring," she explained, looking back on her busy first months in Saint Paul. "[We were] bringing in a business-like atmosphere, re-instilling pride in the musicians, and trying to get the orchestra to more clearly focus on what its goals were."

Borda believed the SPCO needed to reestablish its identity after years in Zukerman's shadow, and she insisted that all fundraising efforts focus on what she considered the orchestra's unique attributes. An early pitch to potential endowment campaign donors reflected her approach.

> *The Saint Paul Chamber Orchestra's principal commitment is to the maintenance of the highest quality of music and performance standards as one of the world's renowned chamber ensembles. Although it shares the marketplace with a symphony orchestra, the organization sees itself as an intimate ensemble capable of presenting a broad repertoire of important work ranging from the baroque to the contemporary. It is the intent of the organization to preserve this unique chamber ensemble identity, and this is viewed as pivotal to the successful realization of its mission.*

Still, as Borda soon discovered, the leaders of many of the area's biggest corporations and foundations remained unconvinced that the SPCO was worthy of major financial support. After separate meetings with representatives of the Bush Foundation and the Dayton-Hudson Foundation, she concluded the orchestra would probably not be able to make any significant progress toward its fundraising goals until two things happened: The SPCO needed to convince funders that it had solved its financial problems, and, perhaps even more important, it needed to answer what Borda called "the music director question."

Borda had moved swiftly in naming Skrowaczewski the orchestra's interim music advisor, but she wasn't about to rush her decision on a permanent replacement for Zukerman. She was determined to find someone who understood and appreciated the SPCO's unique "artistic and financial parameters." Complicating matters, at least two other major orchestras—Cleveland and Pittsburgh—also were looking for new music directors.

By the end of the summer of 1987, Borda went to the board of directors with her recommendation—and it was a jaw dropper. She had decided the SPCO needed not one but three conductors to fill the vacant music director position. Not only that, she knew exactly who those three conductors should be.

Christopher Hogwood, whose streamlined, energetic recordings of Baroque and Classical works had made him a superstar in the Early Music movement, would assume the title director of music and would oversee the orchestra's artistic programming and policies.

The three members of the SPCO's new "artistic commission:" John Adams. Christopher Hogwood, and Hugh Wolff.

Hugh Wolff, the music director of the New Jersey Symphony, would be named principal conductor and would be responsible for the auditioning and promotion of musicians.

John Adams, whose opera, *Nixon in China,* was scheduled to premiere in a few weeks, would occupy the team's third position, creative chair. He would guide the orchestra's selection of contemporary and commissioned works, organize a New Music series, and conduct at least one week of subscription performances.

To Borda's relief, the board of directors loved the idea.

The announcement of the SPCO's new "artistic commission" (or triumvirate or troika or tricycle—everyone seemed to have a favorite name) generated publicity nationwide. As far as anyone knew, no major American orchestra had split up its music directorship among three conductors. Borda was convinced that the time was right for a new approach. "Models evolve to conform to the situation that exists," she told the *New York Times.* "We think the arrangement is in keeping with the orchestra's tradition of innovation. We could have engaged a single director, but we thought this was an exciting approach."

The music world buzzed with speculation about the artistic commission's chances of success. Would the three members of the triumvirate get along? Could the orchestra achieve a cohesive sound under such a diffuse leadership arrangement? ("[The musicians] were very worried about that," Borda later acknowledged.) Would other orchestras around the country follow the SPCO's example? Some critics applauded the SPCO for its audaciousness. Others remained skeptical. "Orchestras would be better off ... to do what they have always done best," the *New York Times'* Donal Henehan grumbled. "Further time-sharing and splintering may only hasten the real revolution: the end of an orchestral tradition that survived nicely for centuries until we came along."

Three in One

As the 1987-1988 season progressed under the interim leadership of Stanislaw Skrowaczewski, the members of the SPCO's new artistic commission tried to figure out how to make their three-way marriage of convenience work. Early on, it became clear it would be difficult to get all three together in the same place. None lived anywhere close to Saint Paul. Christopher Hogwood was based in London, Hugh Wolff lived in New York, and John Adams worked out of San Francisco. Their first scheduled meeting in October turned into a twosome when Adams canceled to attend rehearsals for the *Nixon in China* premiere. "We stepped gingerly around many areas of his responsibility," Wolff reported." The three men held subsequent meetings in New York, Boston, and London, but a canceled flight forced Adams to miss a Saint Paul news conference announcing the troika's debut concert schedule.

The planning process for the artistic commission's first season was significantly less fraught than many insiders and outsiders thought it would be. "I thought we were potentially going to be at each other's throats," Hogwood said, "but things went smoothly." Borda oversaw the process, but left most artistic decisions to the three conductors. "Deborah took a really wise role in coordinating the work of the artistic commission, but not crushing it with her artistic stand," Borda's second-in-command, Brent Assink, said. "She and I worked together to make sure that the seasons were put together and that we brought in the right guest conductors and guest artists and so forth."

The artistic commission's first season schedule promised a clean break with the orchestra's recent past. Common themes—including, most notably, music with links to late-eighteenth-century Paris—would run throughout the concert season. Contemporary music would be a regular feature of the main subscription series, not just the special New Music programs. Above all, the triumvirate would avoid all "grossly overplayed" works. In fact, Wolff said, he and his colleagues had declared "a one-year moratorium on the symphonies of Beethoven and the *Brandenburg Concertos* of Bach."

The first concert of the artistic commission's debut season took place at the Ordway on September 16, 1988—an all-Mozart affair conducted by Hogwood. The *Minneapolis*

Director of Music Christopher Hogwood was one of the world's leading proponents of "historically informed" Baroque and Classical music performances.

Star Tribune's Michael Anthony observed that the sound Hogwood pulled from the orchestra featured "clear, precise, slightly dry textures, strong beats, restrained string vibrato, prominent woodwinds, brisk tempos and strict observance of such matters as repeat signs." In other words, it was about as far away as one could imagine from the luxurious sounds that the orchestra had produced under Pinchas Zukerman. One other obvious difference: Hogwood encouraged the audience to applaud between movements as concertgoers during Mozart's time would have.

Hogwood's debut reflected the nuanced approach that he took throughout the rest of the season. Although he had long championed "authentic" performances of Baroque and Classical music, he did not try to turn the SPCO into an ancient-music ensemble playing period instruments. Instead, he encouraged his musicians to play in a way that was true to the past. "I think period-music people—perhaps unintentionally—promoted the idea that one was aiming at one type of performance that would define everything,"

Principal Conductor Hugh Wolff was widely praised for his creative programming and solid technique.

he said. "The truth is you can adopt an historically aware approach but still have an enormous amount of choices to make that are not spelled out for you by history and about which you can change your mind."

About a month after Hogwood conducted his first concert as the SPCO's director of music, principal conductor Hugh Wolff made his debut. Wolff had promised programs built around common themes, and his first concert of the season did not disappoint. All but one of the pieces on the program were written by French composers and the other—Mozart's Symphony No. 31—was subtitled "Paris." "Wolff has an easy way with this music," critic Michael Anthony observed. "He understands the style—the clarity it needs, the way in which its phrases need to be turned and the way in which its accents and downbeats need to be struck with subtlety (as opposed to the standard German um-pah-pah)."

The imaginative programming and solid technique that Wolff displayed during his first concert of the season served him well as the year progressed. Although he was ostensibly the second among equals in the SPCO triumvirate, there was a widespread assumption that he wouldn't stay second for long. "Many music-business experts, both local and national, are betting on Wolff to pull ahead of the pack, to become, sooner or later, the music director of the orchestra," *Saint Paul Pioneer Press* critic Michael Fleming wrote. "It is too soon to make predictions, but on the basis of Friday night's concert, the SPCO at least has a solid conductor in its stable, one with imagination and flair."

The third member of the artistic commission, John Adams, didn't make his SPCO debut until the following February, but most of the people who showed up for his first concert at the newly refurbished World Theater in Saint Paul seemed to think it was worth the wait. Adams, who had been saddled with the unfortunate title, "creative chair,"

("I'm doing my best to rename my position here") was the troika's designated New Music specialist and he dived into his duties with relish. Although he could easily have included one of his own compositions, he chose instead to feature music by four very different composers—Michael Torke, Alfred Schnittke, Elliott Carter, and Morton Feldman. "[Adams] appeared as a confident conductor and fluent commentator," Michael Fleming wrote.

In the weeks that followed, Adams further strengthened his position within the troika. His second concert—a program featuring excerpts from *Nixon in China* and his new work for baritone and orchestra, the SPCO-commissioned *The Wound-Dresser*—allowed him to display his composing and conducting talents simultaneously. The *Pioneer Press's* Michael Fleming, commenting on Adams's first two appearances with the SPCO, was thoroughly impressed. "Though John Adams has been all along an essential member of the Saint Paul Chamber Orchestra's Artistic Commission," he wrote, "it has only recently become apparent just how powerful a creative force he is on the local scene."

The SPCO's grand, three-headed experiment seemed to be working. In his postmortem on the triumvirate's first season, Michael Fleming gushed that the orchestra under Hogwood, Wolff, and Adams was a free ranging "daredevil driver, accelerator pressed to the floor." The following season he declared: "These are glory days for the Saint Paul Chamber Orchestra." The orchestra and its artistic commission were indeed making beautiful music together, but there was just one problem: The triumvirate was not built to last.

Although Hogwood, Wolff, and Adams were the SPCO's new marquee names, those who looked closely could tell that the one person most responsible for holding the triumvirate together was Deborah Borda. Board chairman Dan Pennie, for one, was convinced that the artistic commission would never succeed without a leader, like Borda, who was "extremely knowledgeable in the business, strong and diplomatic." Several critics pointed out that Borda was not so much a traditional American orchestra president as she was a modern-day version of a European *intendant*—a non-conducting music director who did everything from raising funds, to managing staff, to helping formulate the orchestra's artistic vision. She had developed the artistic commission concept and was its most vocal and effective proponent. She was essential to the troika's long-term viability.

Two weeks into the orchestra's first season with the triumvirate, Borda announced that she would leave the SPCO at the beginning of 1989 to become executive director of the struggling Detroit Symphony. (She would go on to serve a relatively short stint at the Minnesota Orchestra and longer tenures at the New York Philharmonic and the Los Angeles Philharmonic.) During her two-plus years with the SPCO, she had balanced the orchestra's budget, kick-started the nearly complete $10 million endowment campaign, negotiated a new musicians' contract with little acrimony, and finalized a three-year recording contract with Decca. Her departure created a leadership vacuum that left her greatest accomplishment—the artistic commission—in limbo.

"I felt like we were very much in a very good place," she said, looking back on the

The SPCO's new president, William Vickery, presided over the dismantling of Deborah Borda's artistic commission.

Composer-conductor John Harbison replaced John Adams as the SPCO's creative chair in 1990.

state of the orchestra after her two years at the helm. "I felt it was onwards and upwards from there.

"It turned out not to be, I guess."

Falling Apart

William Vickery, who replaced Deborah Borda as president of the SPCO, was not an experienced orchestra administrator. Vickery came to Saint Paul from the National Endowment for the Arts, where he had worked for one year as the director of its music program. Before that, he had served as executive vice president of the Aspen Music Festival and assistant dean of the Aspen Music School. He insisted that his lack of experience in running an orchestra would not hinder him. "I like to take the bull by the horns," he said. "One of my strengths is the ability to see problems before they happen, to prevent them from turning into train wrecks."

During his first year and a half with the SPCO, Vickery seemed content to steer the same course that he had inherited from Borda. The triumvirate completed its second season, 1989-1990, as scheduled, to critical acclaim. Composer-conductor John Harbison was named to replace John Adams, whose contract with the SPCO ran out at the end of the season. The triumvirate was alive and well. The books were balanced. Everything seemed to be moving ahead as planned, but all was not what it seemed.

Although Vickery had kept the artistic commission intact with the hiring of John Harbison, his choice flew in the face of Borda's original intent. The creative chair was supposed to be a position filled by rotating artists from various fields—choreography, philosophy, musicology, and who knew what else. Vickery's decision to replace one composer-conductor (Adams) with another composer-conductor (Harbison) struck some critics, including Michael Fleming, as a gutless "sidestep." Vickery further raised questions about his commitment to the creative chair position when he canceled Harbison's entire New Music series for the 1991-1992 season.

Then there was the question of the artistic commission itself. When asked by a reporter to predict what the SPCO would look like in five years, Vickery responded that he "wouldn't be surprised if the orchestra [had] only one conductor by then." Vickery had not been around at the time of the triumvirate's creation and so had no real stake in the concept. Rumors soon began spreading that Vickery planned to scrap the artistic commission and return the orchestra to the standard music director model. At the end of the 1990-1991 season, the rumors proved to be true. The orchestra announced that Hugh Wolff would take over as music director starting with the 1992-1993 season. Christopher Hogwood would assume the title of principal guest conductor. The position of creative chair would vanish. "We think the artistic commission has been a tremendous success," Vickery said. "Hugh's appointment reflects a natural evolution that has taken place within the framework of the artistic commission."

Even as he dismantled the artistic leadership structure that Borda had put in place, Vickery was overseeing a gradual deterioration of the SPCO's finances. In the fall of 1990, the orchestra announced its first operating deficit in four years—more than $400,000—and an accumulated debt topping $600,000. An examination of the books revealed that budget projections—especially projected increases in contributed income and ticket sales—had been wildly optimistic. Finances stabilized the following year, but by the beginning of 1992, the orchestra was facing another potential $400,000 deficit—one that would push its accumulated debt past $1 million.

As they had in the past, the musicians made concessions to help the orchestra climb out of its financial hole. In return for a commitment by the board to raise $150,000 in new contributions, the players agreed to a 5 percent salary giveback and an extra week of concerts with no pay. That extra week made it possible for the orchestra to schedule seven free concerts during May and June 1992, a program packaged under a familiar name from the Dennis Russell Davies era, Music on the Move. Although the orchestra's publicity department presented the program as an example of the SPCO's new commitment to public outreach, the musicians had agreed to donate their time only because the orchestra was in financial trouble. Management was able to raise nearly $30,000 in cash and about $300,000 in in-kind contributions for Music on the Move. The musicians' concessions, when combined with additional cost-cutting measures and a late fundraising push, actually allowed the orchestra to end the year with a small surplus. That surplus masked a much bigger trouble that was soon to come.

The 1992 version of Music on the Move was a short-lived outreach program initiated after the SPCO's musicians agreed to a package of wage concessions.

During the 1992-1993 season (Hugh Wolff's first season as music director), rumblings about the orchestra's deteriorating financial health became impossible to ignore. Ticket sales fell 12 percent and contributions were flat. A European tour in the spring of 1993 proved to be a critical success but a financial loser, with about $100,000 in uncovered costs. A year after making significant concessions to management, the musicians—who were in negotiations on a new contract—were in no mood for further givebacks. "Any time you're in negotiations, the musicians don't want to talk about concessions," Vickery said.

In June 1993, a few days after the final concert of the 1992-1993 season, William Vickery resigned amid reports that SPCO's end-of-the-fiscal-year deficit would be somewhere in the range of $1 million. The news release announcing his resignation made it sound as though he was leaving of his own accord to take a new position with the Florida Philharmonic, but he was pushed. News reports later revealed that the board of directors had told him to start looking for a new job five months before he actually left.

Crisis

The six months that followed Vickery's departure were among the most difficult the SPCO ever faced. The deficit everyone had been anticipating turned out to be larger than expected. The orchestra's accumulated debt was now nearly $1.6 million. Negotiations on a new musicians' contract were on hold. Season ticketholders wondered whether there would be any concerts to attend. With a new season approaching and no leader at the helm, the board recruited John B. Davis, Jr., to step in as the orchestra's interim president. Davis had no experience with orchestras but he was well known in the Twin Cities as a trouble-shooter and problem-solver. In recent years, he had helped turn around several troubled organizations including Macalester College, the Children's Theatre Company, and the Minneapolis school system. It would be his job to pull the SPCO back from the brink of financial ruin.

The musicians had five days to approve a new contract recognizing the artistic alliance between the SPCO, the Ordway, and the opera.

At the end of August 1993, about a month after taking over as interim president, Davis made a major announcement: The SPCO was joining the Ordway Music Theatre and the Minnesota Opera in an artistic alliance to consolidate operations, cut costs, and increase artistic cooperation. The centerpiece of the alliance was an agreement under which the SPCO would replace the opera company's existing orchestra and essentially become the Ordway's house band. Hugh Wolff had proposed the idea, pointing out that many European opera houses employed resident orchestras with multiple duties. The SPCO board embraced the proposal as a way to reduce costs and increase revenue—but no one bothered to ask the SPCO musicians what they thought.

As soon became clear, the musicians abhorred the idea. Central to their objections was the requirement that they replace the musicians in the Minnesota Opera orchestra, who had been on strike since May. The SPCO musicians already played one production per season with the opera company, but they did not want to take additional work away from their colleagues. "It's not that the Chamber Orchestra musicians think that their participation in some Minnesota Opera productions is entirely untenable," said Liza DeBrul, an attorney for the SPCO players. "But we also cannot be expected to solve the very dysfunctional labor relations of the Minnesota Opera."

On September 10, the day before the 1993-1994 season was scheduled to begin, the SPCO board of directors issued an ultimatum: The musicians had five days to approve a new contract recognizing the artistic alliance between the SPCO, the Ordway, and the opera. If they failed to do so, the orchestra would immediately file for bankruptcy.

The musicians were stunned. "It was total shock and anger and dismay," said horn player Herb Winslow, the musicians' representative on the negotiating committee. "[We thought] we had been left with some room to maneuver in order to reach some kind of a compromise settlement. But this leaves no room for compromise and puts the Chamber Orchestra out of business."

Opening night of the 1993-1994 season was a surreal combination of beautiful music and labor unrest. Outside the Ordway, management served free ice cream to patrons as a Dixieland band tried its best to create a festive mood. Nearby, musicians handed out leaflets that stated their case.

> *Saint Paul Chamber Orchestra musicians have sacrificed repeatedly to preserve our orchestra and to avoid labor disputes. Morally, legally and ethically, we cannot and will not permit ourselves to be used as nasty pawns in the labor dispute of another organization! Doing so would make a mockery of our spotless record of labor peace, and still wouldn't solve the Saint Paul Chamber Orchestra's board and management problems.*

The small crowd that showed up for the opening night performance (about one third of the seats were empty) gave the orchestra a prolonged standing ovation before the first note was played. Once the applause died down, Hugh Wolff turned to the house, welcomed the audience to the beginning of the orchestra's thirty-fifth anniversary season and then added, "May it not be its last."

With little desire to actually follow through on its bankruptcy threat (no bankruptcy documents were ever drawn up), the board of directors pushed back its deadline. Two weeks later, the two sides reached a deal. The musicians would give up more than $800,000 over the next four years by agreeing to shorter seasons and a reduction in the number of players—from thirty-four to thirty-two. The musicians also agreed to play no more than two opera performances each season. The settlement effectively killed the artistic alliance between the SPCO, the Ordway, and the Minnesota Opera, but Hugh Wolff, the man who proposed the idea in the first place, didn't seem to mind. "We have our house in order and a sense of where we're going and how we're going to get there," he said.

What Wolff failed to acknowledge was that the SPCO still had a $1.6 million accumulated deficit and no clear plan for getting rid of it. The agreement with the musicians had prompted First Bank of Saint Paul to restore the SPCO's suspended line of credit, but the orchestra estimated it would run out of money to pay its bills by early December. Carl Drake Jr., the chairman of the board of the Saint Paul-based Bigelow Foundation and a member of the Ordway board, spoke for many when he expressed skepticism about the orchestra's chances for survival. "I don't think there are going to be a lot of people running to the fore to shore up an operation in the red," he said. "There have already been several rescues in the last fifteen years. They're trying to go out and raise what I call dead-horse money."

To the Rescue

For years, the SPCO's musicians had lamented what they considered a general lack of appreciation for the orchestra among the people of Saint Paul. The feeling of being

Minnesota Public Radio's S.O.S. ("Save Our SPCO") radiothon reached beyond the airwaves to the streets of Saint Paul.

Garrison Keillor, shown here during a performance with the SPCO at Saint Paul's World Theater, was among the talents who helped make the thirty-five-hour fund drive a success.

unappreciated was often most acute when they returned from tours—tours on which they often were treated as celebrities—and discovered that few people back home seemed to have noticed they were gone. The SPCO had a devoted fan base, but that base was relatively small. There was little evidence to suggest that support for the orchestra was widespread. Then again, no one had ever really asked the community to show its support.

By the middle of October, the orchestra's line of credit was dwindling by the day. Funders were reluctant to give any more money to an organization that had recently threatened to declare bankruptcy. It was hard to imagine where the SPCO would get the funds it needed to stay afloat.

At Minnesota Public Radio, Michael Barone—who had hosted and produced SPCO broadcasts for nearly two decades—monitored the orchestra's travails with growing concern. "I was kind of the nervous chicken little running around here saying the sky is about to fall," he later recalled. "I was very close to those people [at the orchestra] and their music, and when they got into that financial dead end it looked really horrible." Barone went to his boss, MPR president Bill Kling, and together the two men hatched a plan to help the SPCO: MPR would stage an on-the-air fundraiser similar to the pledge drives it regularly aired to refill its own coffers—only this time the money raised would go directly to the orchestra.

"It seems clear that without funds, the orchestra's time will run out," Kling said in a statement announcing his plans for the fundraiser. "We hope that MPR's listeners around the region can provide the financial assistance the SPCO needs to continue operations through the end of the fiscal year."

Federal regulations prohibited public broadcasters from raising money for outside organizations, so MPR asked the Federal Communications Commission for a waiver. The FCC had granted such an exemption only twice before: in 1982, for the rebuilding of the National Symphony's fire-gutted summer home, Wolf Trap; and in 1989, for recovery efforts following the San Francisco earthquake. Two weeks after receiving MPR's request, the FCC granted the waiver.

MPR's S.O.S. ("Save Our SPCO") radiothon started at 6 a.m. on the morning of Friday, October 29, 1993, and ran until 5 p.m. the following day. Pitches for donations shared time with recordings from the SPCO archives, live performances by SPCO ensembles, interviews with musical celebrities (including Pinchas Zukerman), and original broadcasts of Garrison Keillor's "Young Lutherans' Guide to the Orchestra." During the thirty-five hours the fund drive was on the air, MPR received more than 5,300 pledges totaling nearly $750,000. Going into the weekend, Bill Kling had estimated that the radiothon would raise perhaps $100,000. "It turns out the community just surprised everyone," he said.

After years of wondering whether they truly had the community's widespread support, the musicians of the SPCO—and all the people who worked with them—now knew that they were indeed appreciated. "The radiothon was the most important nonmusical event in the SPCO's history," Hugh Wolff said. "It is certainly the most exciting thing that has happened since I've been involved with the orchestra. Each of us as an individual was made to realize that there was such a great level of support and concern and generosity in the community."

With the sudden and unexpected infusion of three-quarters of a million community-donated dollars, the SPCO was well on its way to financial recovery. A large chunk of the $1.6 million accumulated deficit still remained, but the community's overwhelming show of support during the radiothon had raised new hopes that the SPCO had indeed weathered its worst crisis and that the board of directors would find ways to build on the momentum. "By opening its checkbooks, the community has driven the wolves temporarily from the SPCO's door," the editors of the *Saint Paul Pioneer Press* wrote. "Now it's time for the [SPCO] board to put up a sturdy fence so they don't return."

The S.O.S. phone bank took in nearly $750,000 in pledges.

Musical Journey

With all the problems facing the SPCO during the summer and fall of 1993, it was easy to forget that the orchestra was still making beautiful music and that its newly promoted music director, Hugh Wolff, was leading the ensemble in directions it had never gone before. Central to Wolff's vision was an elaborate, eight-year programming sequence that he called "Music on the Move: A Tour of the Centuries." In this case, Music on Move involved moving the orchestra not from place to place, but from century to century. Wolff mapped out a detailed plan in which the first eight years of the post-triumvirate era were split into four two-season segments. Each segment paired the music of a particular century with the music from a particular twenty-five-year period of the 1900s. Thus, during his first two seasons as music director (1992-1993 and 1993-1994), Wolff combined music from 1600 to 1700 with music written between the years 1900 and 1925. "The Music on the Move idea is a scaffold for us to build upon, a way to program music in a more interesting way," he explained. "It gives us a chance to look into the nooks and crannies of the chamber music repertoire and see what we've missed."

During a survey of previous programming, Wolff discovered the orchestra had missed quite a bit of music over the years. For example, it had played less than half of Haydn's 106 symphonies and only about a dozen of the forty-one written by Mozart. Wolff sensed an opportunity to expose the orchestra and its audience to seldom-played music that deserved to be heard. "It doesn't mean playing less valuable or less interesting music," he explained, "but certainly with a chamber orchestra, where there is so much music you *cannot* play, it means making sure there isn't music you *can* play that you've neglected."

Although Wolff built his seasons around the Tour of the Centuries format, he did not limit his musical choices to designated periods. The concept was, instead, a device that helped him organize his thoughts and unearth neglected repertoire. "In general, I've always found thematic programming useful," he said, "if only for me, rather than for the audience."

Wolff's creative approach to programming included a willingness to collaborate with other performing arts organizations. In the fall of 1994, the Martha Graham Dance Company joined the SPCO for a performance celebrating the fiftieth anniversary of the premiere of Aaron Copland's *Appalachian Spring* (the composition that headlined the SPCO's 1980 Grammy Award-winning album). Copland had written the piece as a ballet scored for thirteen instruments but, over the years, audiences had grown accustomed to hearing it in full symphonic garb. The collaboration between the SPCO and the Graham company sought to recreate the excitement that had accompanied the piece's debut fifty years earlier. Wolff was delighted with the results.

> *They had a videotape of the original choreography and that was, for me, revelatory. Finally I understood what everything in the score meant, because you could see the action. Every note was written from Martha's choreography and all her choreography was designed with [Copland's] notes [in mind] ... We played the videotape and [the musicians] really got into it. Where else would you have the chance to do that? Where else would that be as important as it was here, since that was a signature piece of the orchestra?*

A stop along the way on the SPCO's spring 1993 European tour.

Not all collaborations were as successful as the *Appalachian Spring* performance. During the second half of a concert in the fall of 1996, the SPCO teamed up with Minneapolis's Theatre de la Jeune Lune to present what *Minneapolis Star Tribune* reviewer Michael Anthony called a "bizarre" staging of Mozart's mini-opera, *The Impresario*. Mozart's story of two operatic prima donnas was recast as an audition for a television commercial, with the SPCO playing the role of a studio band. "It was all quite engaging," Anthony wrote, "a prime example of imagination run amok."

Still, despite the occasional creative overreach, Wolff was establishing a comfortable rapport with the orchestra and the orchestra was, in turn, producing some of the best music it had ever made. European tours in 1993 and 1997 and a first-ever visit to Japan in 1996 garnered glowing reviews and further raised the orchestra's international profile. Annual national tours included stops at prestigious venues such as Carnegie Hall and Avery Fisher Hall in New York, Symphony Hall in Boston, Orchestra Hall in Chicago, and Davies Hall in San Francisco. In addition, the orchestra was setting a torrid recording pace under Wolff's direction—one that would ultimately produce nineteen recordings for the Teldec and Virgin Classics labels. "This group ... under the direction of Hugh Wolff, has developed an effortlessly polished sound," *New York Times* critic Alex

Ross wrote. "The various sections are well balanced, the ensemble exact, [and] Mr. Wolff shapes his interpretations with impeccable taste."

Recovery

As the orchestra flourished artistically under Hugh Wolff, the business side of the operation rebounded impressively from its near death experience in the summer and fall of 1993. Much of the credit for the SPCO's recovery went to the orchestra's new president and managing director, Brent Assink. Assink had risen through the SPCO's administrative ranks during the 1980s, but left in 1990 to become general manager of the San Francisco Symphony. When the SPCO first approached him about filling the vacancy left by William Vickery, he wasn't sure he wanted the job. The orchestra was, after all, in the middle of a financial crisis that seemed destined to result in bankruptcy. Then MPR came to the rescue with its radiothon. Assink was so impressed by the community's response that he put aside his initial misgivings and accepted the SPCO position. "There is no doubt—if the radiothon hadn't happened, I wouldn't have come here," he said. "It bought us some time to get our house in order and to raise more money."

The SPCO's prodigious recording output under Hugh Wolff continued into the new century with a new CD featuring the talents of cellist Yo-Yo Ma and bassist Edgar Meyer.

Assink rejoined the SPCO in early 1994 and immediately set out to restore the orchestra's downtrodden image with the public and institutional funders. He recruited Gary Woeltge to fill the board's vacant chairmanship when no one else would accept the responsibility. He streamlined the board's executive committee to make it more efficient. He rebuilt the orchestra's administrative staff, which had been ravaged by layoffs. He extended Hugh Wolff's contract and named pop vocalist Bobby McFerrin the orchestra's new "creative chair." He also launched a new education program called CONNECT (Chamber Orchestra's Neighborhood Network of Education, Curriculum, and Teachers) to strengthen the orchestra's outreach efforts, better utilize the musicians' time, and raise more institutional money. "I was certainly focused on rebuilding the institution," Assink later recalled. "The number of sleepless nights I had about the finances was just incredible."

Saint Paul Mayor Norm Coleman congratulates President and Managing Director Brent Assink on the opening of the new Saint Paul Chamber OrcheSTORE, a one-stop retail establishment featuring "tickets, recordings, and more."

The addition of Bobby McFerrin turned out to be a particularly savvy move. McFerrin was a nine-time Grammy winner best known for his astonishing vocalizations. (He was often described as a one-man vocal ensemble.) He also was a classically trained pianist who had long been fascinated by the art of conducting. He had taken up the craft in 1990, and since then had worked with more than forty orchestras, including those in San Francisco, Los Angeles, Pittsburgh, Detroit, Dallas, and Atlanta. In February 1994, he debuted with the SPCO as a guest conductor. Afterward, the orchestra's assistant

SPCO Principal Trumpet Gary Bordner visits first-grade students at Minneapolis's Longfellow Early Education Center as part of the CONNECT education program, 1995.

concertmaster, Leslie Shank, approached him with a proposal.

"There's an associate conductor's job open," she said. "Are you interested?"

"Not a bit," he answered."

But the more McFerrin thought about it, the more the idea appealed to him. Back in San Francisco, where he made his home, he went to see Brent Assink, who was getting ready to move back to Saint Paul. Their meeting resulted in a decision to have McFerrin fill the "creative chair" position that had been vacant since John Harbison left in 1992. It was an unconventional hiring—the sort that invited criticism from classical music purists—but Assink was convinced that McFerrin would help the SPCO bounce back from its recent troubles. "We hired Bobby to give us as much visibility as he could," Assink admitted.

McFerrin's first concert as creative chair prompted wildly divergent responses from local and national music critics. The *Saint Paul Pioneer Press's* Michael Fleming was among the least impressed. "There is no use pretending that [McFerrin] is more than a novice conductor," he wrote. "His lack of stick technique ... [made] any attempt by the players to phrase useless." The *Minneapolis Star Tribune's* Michael Anthony, however, seemed more willing to look beyond McFerrin's "unconventional" baton work. "[It] appeared to make sense to the orchestra," he observed. "Judging by his body language and by the cues he gave, it seemed clear that McFerrin not only gets on well with the orchestra but that he was eminently familiar with the music at hand, all of which he conducted without a score."

Bobby McFerrin's arrival in Saint Paul created a sustained buzz among national news media outlets.

McFerrin's arrival in Saint Paul generated unprecedented publicity for the orchestra, including long articles in the *New York Times* and *Wall Street Journal,* and a half-hour profile on ABC-TV's *Nightline.* Much of the coverage focused on McFerrin's work with the orchestra's new public school outreach program, CONNECT. During the program's official kickoff at Saint Paul's Dayton's Bluff Elementary in early 1995, a slew of reporters marveled at the dreadlocked conductor's ability to make music fun. The *Star Tribune's* Michael Anthony was particularly taken with McFerrin's willingness to play along with his young audience, as he did during a let's-make-up-a-song demonstration.

After gathering sonic ideas from the audience—high squeaks in the strings, whirling figures in the woodwinds— McFerrin asked what key the piece should be in. "H!" shouted a boy seated on the floor near the front.

Undaunted, McFerrin turned to the orchestra, said, "Gimme an H," hit a downbeat, and the players put forth a blaring, wildly cacophonous noise that drew a cheer from the audience.

Bobby McFerrin and the SPCO perform for first-grade students at Groveland Park Elementary School in Saint Paul, 1995.

A House Divided

The addition of Bobby McFerrin increased the SPCO's "coolness" quotient, helped boost ticket sales, and made it at least a bit easier for Brent Assink to focus on other challenges facing the orchestra. By the mid-1990s, few problems were more vexing than the orchestra's increasingly acrimonious relationship with the Ordway Music Theatre.

The SPCO's problems with the Ordway dated back to the theater's creation in the 1980s. Originally conceived as a modest playhouse, the Ordway had evolved—with significant encouragement from Pinchas Zukerman—into an ornate, something-for-everyone theater with four "principal users"—the SPCO, the Minnesota Opera, the Schubert Club, and the Minnesota Orchestra. Cost overruns during construction had scuttled plans to raise an endowment and had saddled the theater with $9 million in long-term debt. As a result, the Ordway's management spent the better part of five years trying to develop a formula that would allow it to balance its considerable financial needs with those of its primary tenants.

The formula on which the Ordway eventually settled—a growing reliance on Broadway touring productions—made life increasingly difficult for the SPCO. In the spring of 1993, the orchestra had to juggle its concert schedule to accommodate a twelve-week run of Andrew Lloyd Webber's *The Phantom of the Opera.* The money lost as a result of the rescheduling contributed to the financial crisis of the following summer and autumn. In the fall of 1995, the SPCO had to delay for one month the start of its 1995-1996 season while the blockbuster musical, *Show Boat,* finished its twelve-week Ordway run. The *Show Boat* fiasco infuriated Brent Assink and he vented his frustration in a widely circulated memo to Kenneth Dayton of the Dayton-Hudson Foundation. "I want to you to know that I am outraged by what I understand the Ordway has done to the Saint Paul Chamber Orchestra," he wrote. "If you have a contract [with the Ordway], I hope you will force them to abide by it."

Hugh Wolff, Christopher Hogwood, and the SPCO strike a pose outside the orchestra's primary concert venue, the Ordway Music Theatre, 1990.

A new five-year license agreement signed in early 1996 solidified the SPCO's claim to approximately sixty Ordway concert dates a year, but the deal failed to significantly reduce tensions between the two organizations. By 1998, the managers of the orchestra and the Ordway were bickering more vehemently than they ever had before—this time, over an Ordway proposal to accommodate more opera productions by reducing or eliminating the SPCO's Wednesday evening Baroque Series performances. "The Ordway is not worried about the political fallout or trying to adjust the principal users' schedule," Assink wrote in a memo summarizing the ongoing negotiations. "The Ordway now feels that they must just do what they think is the best thing and let the chips fall where they may." It appeared that it could be many more years before the two organizations worked out their differences.

Multiple Codas

In February 1998, Hugh Wolff announced that he would step down as the SPCO's music director at the close of the 1999-2000 season. "What gave me the confidence that this was the right thing was that the orchestra's really in good shape, artistically and financially," he said. In the twenty-seven months following his announcement, the orchestra experienced a string of goings and comings that made it clear one era was ending and another was beginning.

In April 1998, Christopher Hogwood led his last concert as the orchestra's principal guest conductor. He had come to the SPCO ten years earlier as the unofficial head of Deborah Borda's three-man artistic commission. His responsibilities with the orchestra had diminished over the years, but Saint Paul had remained a large part of his life. "There have been no major disasters," he said, "and a lot of nice—I think—friendly and cooperative music-making."

Two months after Hogwood left, Romuald Tecco played his last concert as the orchestra's concertmaster. Tecco had come to Saint Paul in 1972 with his friend, Dennis Russell Davies, and had been a mainstay with the SPCO ever since. As a tribute to his twenty-six years, the orchestra presented him with a book featuring words of affection and admiration from his many fans—including a twenty-nine-year-old woman with a long memory.

*My first orchestral experience was about 23 years
ago, when Mom "dragged" me to hear SPCO at
Christmastime. We had front-row seats. I had no idea
of the great magnitude of performer/artist you are.
I sat right in front of you, and as I "harumphed"
from clapping for so long, you laughed, smiled and
winked. Because of that I keep returning, and when
I feel distracted, your fingers and grace bring me back
to the music.*

In the spring of 1999, Brent Assink stepped down as SPCO
president to accept a similar position with the San Francisco
Symphony. Assink had overseen the orchestra's recovery from
its 1993 near-collapse. He had restored the SPCO's battered
reputation and balanced its books five years in a row. Board
Chair Terry Saario believed Assink was leaving the orchestra in
remarkably good shape. "If I could clone him, I would clone
him," she said.

On May 27, 2000, Hugh Wolff conducted his final concert
as music director of the SPCO. Wolff stuck with the orchestra
through its darkest days and had presided over an eight-year "Tour
of the Centuries" that highlighted his programming creativity. He
had led more than five hundred concerts, more than any other
SPCO conductor. He had guided the orchestra on three major
overseas tours and made nineteen recordings. Wolff closed out
his twelve-year SPCO run with Beethoven's powerful Symphony
No. 9. There was little fanfare—certainly nothing like the farewell
gala that had marked the end of the Pinchas Zukerman era. Wolff
didn't seem to mind. At intermission, he received words of praise
from the orchestra's board and a Minnesota Senate proclamation in
his honor. Then he turned to the audience. "I just want to say," he
started, then paused and sighed, "that it was really an honor and a
privilege to have had this job. It's been twelve gorgeous years. We
couldn't have done it without you—we've done it for you. With
Beethoven gloriously ringing in our ears, we're trying to take you
somewhere you haven't been before. I thank you from the bottom
of my heart."

Romuald Tecco and Hugh Wolff.

Applause for the outgoing music director.
Standing left to right: Board Chair John
Huss, Saint Paul Mayor Norm Coleman,
the SPCO's new president and managing
director, Bruce Coppock, and Hugh Wolff.

Hugh Wolff
Principal Conductor, 1988-1992
Music Director, 1992-2000

After seven years with the mercurial Pinchas Zukerman, The Saint Paul Chamber Orchestra was ready for a conductor who was, if not more predictable, then at least more reassuringly steady in his technique and temperament. Few conductors fit that description better than Hugh Wolff.

Although he joined the SPCO at the young age of thirty-five, his rise to the heights of his profession was not so much meteoric as it was deliberate. Unlike many of his contemporaries, he had been slow to choose his musical path. He spent four years at Harvard, pursuing a composition major. ("I didn't know what I wanted then," he said.) While he was there, he got his first taste of conducting. From then on, he was hooked. His first big break came in 1979 when he was selected as the ExxonArts Endowment conductor of the National Symphony Orchestra. That appointment led to a series of increasingly prestigious positions: music director of the Northeastern Pennsylvania Philharmonic associate conductor of the National Symphony and music director of the New Jersey Symphony. In Saint Paul, he continued his steady climb by first assuming the position of principal conductor of the SPCO's artistic commission and then ascending to music director.

"I would like people to think of what I have done over the last ten years as a paradigm for the young American conductor," he explained in 1992. "My career shows it's possible to move up in a very traditional, stepwise way from a metropolitan to a regional to a big-city orchestra. Not so many of my own colleagues, even the ones who are my age, are doing that."

Wolff's press clippings often noted his lack of pretensions—at least when compared to other top-notch conductors. The *Baltimore Sun* described him as "lanky, freckled and red-haired ... a grown-up version of the boy next door." Others marveled at what they perceived to be his undersized (for a major conductor) ego. "Take [his] enthusiastic embrace of [Bobby] McFerrin as SPCO creative chair," *Minnesota Monthly's* Eric Friesen wrote in 1996. "A lesser, and less secure, music director might have been threatened by the arrival of a pop superstar as his new colleague and might have used all of the devices in his power to foil the plan from the start ... Not so Wolff."

Wolff's reviews were often similarly flattering. The *Washington Post* reported during Wolff's second season as the SPCO's music director that he "is now imprinting his unique and elegant style on this talented group." The *New York Times* observed that he "shapes his interpretations with impeccable taste."

Wolff's relationship with his musicians featured fewer peaks and valleys than that of his predecessor, but his departure after twelve years was timely—if not overdo. When Brent Assink proposed to the musicians that Wolff stay on for an extra year while the search for his successor continued, the musicians made it clear that they preferred to bring in an interim music director. "I think he picked the right time to leave," veteran horn player Herb Winslow said at the beginning of Wolff's final season with the SPCO. "A conductor gets to a point where's he's made all the changes he wants to make in an ensemble, and you've had a great success with it. But you don't want to keep doing the same thing. And from a musician's standpoint, we get used to a conductor. After a certain point, you hear him say the same thing about a Haydn symphony or whatever, and it becomes day-to-day."

Wolff left the SPCO for a prestigious position as principal conductor of Germany's Frankfurt Radio Symphony. After five years living in London and working throughout Europe, he and his family—his wife, writer and harpist Judith Kogan, and their three sons—moved back to the Twin Cities in 2005. His long-range goals include an affiliation with a major U.S. orchestra.

"That's what I hope would happen over the next few years," he said.

Review

Dvořák: Serenade in E for Strings, op. 22. Serenade in D Minor for Two Oboes, Two Clarinets, Two Bassoons, Contrabassoon, Three Horns, Cello, and Double bass, op. 44; The Saint Paul Chamber Orchestra, Hugh Wolff conducting.

One's first impression from this disc is likely to be of the incredibly rich and beautiful cellos in the opening measures of the string serenade, but that is only the first of a host of felicities showered upon the listener. Conductor Hugh Wolff presents a clear overall picture of Dvořák's two serenades, all the while enhancing each with a constant stream of subtle but telling inflections and subtleties, resulting in radiant performances of some of the most winning music in the repertoire for chamber orchestras. One reason why this pairing is so appealing is that it divides the orchestra into its major constituent parts and gives each an opportunity to show its mettle. The opportunity is not lost on the members of the Saint Paul Chamber Orchestra, whose play is superlative in both works. The recording is superbly transparent, but well balanced, warm, and natural. Of the now six disc versions of this pairing, I would judge Wolff's to be the most desirable. His wind serenade, especially in the heartbreaking *Andante con moto*, is among the best in any format.

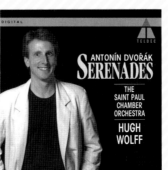

This disc is one of four that comprise Wolff's recording debut with the Saint Paul Chamber Orchestra for Teldec. If the others are at all comparable, this is a most auspicious beginning. As a Jerseyite I must confess to having a special interest in this development, since Wolff used to be with the home team—that is, the New Jersey Symphony. So we'll be following his career, much like fans of a ball player who has switched uniforms, and telling everybody that we told you so.

—*Fanfare,* March/April 1992

Chapter Five
Grand Experiment

———————

Even before the musicians took the Ordway stage on the evening of October 22, 2004, it was evident to anyone with a keen eye that that times were changing at The Saint Paul Chamber Orchestra. The players' chairs and music stands were all in place, just as they always were, but something was missing. The podium.

The musicians filed in, assembled, and tuned their instruments. Then, after a moment of silence, the audience erupted in applause as Joshua Bell took his place onstage. Bell was by many accounts the most acclaimed violinist of his generation—a virtuoso of incomparable talent and boy-next-door good looks. (Not surprisingly, the packed house seemed to skew younger and perhaps a tad more female than the usual SPCO crowd.) Bell had appeared as a soloist with the orchestra on several occasions; now he was trying something different.

With a nod and a flick of his bow, Bell launched the orchestra into the familiar opening allegro of Vivaldi's *The Four Seasons.* Soon it was clear that he and the orchestra had no need for a podium—or a baton for that matter. They progressed through Vivaldi's spring, summer, autumn, and winter in synchronized unity. Flutist Julia Bogorad-Kogan provided a kind of running commentary, narrating the composer's accompanying sonnets at appropriate breaks in the movements. With the piece's final, shivering allegro and Bogorad-Kogan's closing pronouncement ("This is winter, but it brings joy"), it was hard not to wonder why the orchestra had ever bothered to work with a conductor in the first place.

> Soon it was clear that he and the orchestra had no need for a podium—or a baton for that matter.

The second half of the program raised the conductor-or-no-conductor question even more forcefully. Bell joined the orchestra for a virtuoso, four-minute performance of Mozart's Rondo in C—again, without the aid of a podium or baton. Then, as if to underline the superfluous nature of his leadership, he walked offstage, leaving the ensemble to handle Richard Strauss's Suite for Winds on its own. For the finale, he reemerged from the wings, took a seat next to concertmaster Steven Copes, and, from his chair, led the orchestra in a sizzling rendition of the overture from Rossini's *The Barber of Seville.*

Eight months earlier, the SPCO had announced that it was commencing a grand experiment—abandoning its reliance on a single music director and entrusting its onstage leadership to a group of "artistic partners" that included Joshua Bell. In the press coverage leading up to his debut as artistic partner, Bell had taken pains to explain that he was not a standard baton-waving conductor. He preferred to think of himself as a "leader"—a first among equals in an orchestra made up of musical risk-takers. "I just love it," he said of his new leadership role with the SPCO. "These can be some of the most electrifying performances. You feel like every player is sitting on the edge." As the Ordway thundered with applause following the Rossini overture's rousing finale, most members of the orchestra were inclined to agree.

Left: The SPCO performs at one of its neighborhood venues, Wooddale Church in Eden Prairie, 2003.

Stuck

In September 1999, at the start of Hugh Wolff's final season with the SPCO, Bruce Coppock arrived in Saint Paul to replace the departed Brent Assink as the orchestra's president and managing director. Coppock was a former professional cellist and an experienced orchestral administrator. His resume included a five-year stint as executive director of the Saint Louis Symphony and, most recently, the directorship of the American Symphony Orchestra League's Leadership Academy. By most outward appearances, Coppock was taking over an orchestra in remarkably good shape. The SPCO had balanced its budget every year since its near demise in 1993. It had built up its endowment to a respectable level. It was a financially stable ensemble with a solid record of musical accomplishment. But something was amiss.

"I think the orchestra was kind of stuck," Coppock explained years later. "It was living on its reputation from a time when basically it had no competition."

Over the previous two-and-a-half decades, while the SPCO was building a record of considerable artistic achievement, its competition had evolved. Worldwide, the number of top-notch chamber orchestras had multiplied and many of the newcomers were specialty ensembles—Baroque groups, New Music groups, and orchestras concentrating

Bruce Coppock would go on to lead the SPCO as its president and managing director for nine years after his arrival in 1999.

on the Classical repertoire of the eighteenth and nineteenth centuries. The SPCO, meanwhile, had remained true to what Hugh Wolff called its "generalist approach." It was a do-it-all chamber orchestra that took pride in playing many types of music very well. In the chamber orchestra world, the trend was toward specialization. By the turn of the millennium, the SPCO had lost its competitive edge in an increasingly crowded and specialized international chamber music marketplace.

The orchestra's board members did not realize exactly what the problem was, but they sensed that something was wrong and their instructions to their new president and managing director were clear. They told Coppock they wanted him to take the SPCO to the next level—to turn what already was a very good chamber orchestra into "the preeminent chamber orchestra in the world."

Coppock spent much of his first year in Saint Paul trying to figure out how to move the orchestra in the direction the board wanted it to go. He set out to gain a clear understanding of the orchestra's identity and what he found was sobering. "Everybody talked about how the SPCO was a unique organization," he said. "But with very few exceptions—I point to the period of the artistic commission and the heyday of Dennis Davies—it didn't actually look very different. It wasn't very distinctive in terms of what it actually did."

Coppock was beginning to suspect that if the SPCO were truly to make the jump to the next level, it would have to abandon the traditional music director leadership scheme and adopt a new approach—perhaps something akin to Deborah Borda's triumvirate. But he was not ready to make any hasty moves. "It would have been premature to say let's revert to some version of the artistic commission," he explained. "I didn't have a political base here. I was too new to do something so radical." Instead, he moved forward with the search for a new music director to replace Hugh Wolff—a process that was well underway by the time he arrived, but going slower than expected.

Eleven other North American orchestras including the Boston Symphony, the New York Philharmonic, the Philadelphia Orchestra, and the Minnesota Orchestra also were looking for new music directors, and their short lists were all very similar. Since many of the most sought-after candidates were thought to be holding out for jobs with big symphonies, the SPCO had to bide its time. It turned its 2000-2001 season into something of an extended audition, with several potential candidates—among them, Peter Oundjian and Roberto Abbado—taking their place on the Saint Paul podium.

In the end, the audition process proved largely unnecessary. A few weeks into the season, Coppock and the search committee made their choice—a surprising one. The SPCO's new music director would be Andreas Delfs of the Milwaukee Symphony Orchestra.

"A lot of people weren't guessing we were looking at him," horn player Herb Winslow said.

"Andreas was a complete sleeper, "Coppock later admitted. "He was not on the radar screen."

The Delfs Era

German-born Andreas Delfs had all the makings of a superb chamber orchestra conductor. He had worked as an assistant conductor under former SPCO music director Dennis Russell Davies at the Stuttgart Opera and Chamber Orchestra. He had served as music director of the Hannover State Opera and Orchestra. His tenure in Milwaukee was widely deemed a success. He was in growing demand as guest conductor with major orchestras around the United States. He had an engaging personality. The musicians seemed to like him. At a news conference announcing his appointment, Delfs lived up to his reputation as an easy-going and non-conventional maestro. "I want to talk to you today about health care and balancing the federal budget," he told a confused press corps before adding: "No, wait a minute, that's the wrong speech."

"It looked like we had perhaps caught a star ascendant," Coppock said.

"At a time when major orchestras everywhere are looking for fireworks amid the masterworks," the *St. Paul Pioneer Press'* Matt Peiken wrote in early 2001, "The Saint Paul Chamber Orchestra needed [Andreas] Delfs's unabashed daring."

Although Delfs was not scheduled to take over the SPCO's music directorship until the fall of 2001, he wasted little time in capturing the public's attention. During a guest appearance in Saint Paul just three months after his appointment, he strapped an accordion over his shoulder and accompanied the orchestra in a performance of the suite from Kurt Weill's *Threepenny Opera.* Many concertgoers were unsure what to make of a conductor who played an instrument often associated with beer halls and polkas, but they certainly remembered the experience. "It takes a strong guy to be our music director," Herb Winslow laughed afterwards. "I think he showed what he's made of."

Delfs's first season with the SPCO did not go nearly as smoothly as he or the orchestra had hoped it would. Two weeks before Delfs was scheduled to make his concert debut as music director, the terrorist attacks of September 11 forced the orchestra and its audience to confront the meaning of music in the wake of unfathomable human tragedy. In its first concert after the attacks, the orchestra strived to balance conflicting emotions with its unscheduled performances of "Air on the G String" from Bach's Suite No. 3 (after which the audience, sensing the gravity of the moment, intuitively held its applause) and the sprightly "Spring" and "Summer" movements of Vivaldi's *The Four Seasons.* Four weeks later, the SPCO joined the Minnesota Orchestra, the Dale Warland Singers, the Minnesota Chorale, and the chorus of the Plymouth Music Series in a moving benefit concert titled "Elegy" at Orchestra Hall.

The SPCO had hoped to capitalize on the excitement generated by Delfs's arrival, but it never really got the chance. Delfs was disappointed to find that in the aftermath of the terrorist attacks, many concertgoers reacted coolly to what he called his "light touch" to music. "While I think people enjoyed it, I don't think [they enjoyed it] to the degree that I had hoped," he said. Delfs responded by scheduling more "serious music"—Mozart, Bach, and Vivaldi—into the orchestra's main subscription series for the 2002-2003 season.

Even as Delfs worked to reconnect with his audience, his relationship with his musicians was deteriorating. Although many players initially responded favorably to their new music director (principal flutist Julia Bogorad-Kogan called him a "glamorous figure" who could "help people see us as an orchestra playing fun music"), the orchestra was not gelling under his leadership. "At the end of the day, it just didn't click," Coppock explained. "That's not a judgment on the orchestra. It's not a judgment on Delfs. Sometimes chemistry just doesn't work, and this one didn't work."

As the 2001-2002 season came to a close, Coppock faced a difficult decision. The orchestra had placed a considerable bet on Delfs. It plastered his image on almost every available flat surface—billboards, buses, and banners—and had worked up a whimsical ad campaign in which he seemingly was casting for walleye with his baton. It even arranged for the street in front of the Ordway to be temporarily renamed Delfs Drive. Now, after just one season, it appeared that Delfs—the public face of the orchestra—was not going to work out. The question was, what to do next?

A Marriage of Polygamy

Coppock insisted he fully expected Delfs to succeed in Saint Paul, but he had never been comfortable with the orchestra's 2001-2002 Delfs-centered marketing campaign. Even as the season was just getting underway, Coppock publicly expressed misgivings about placing so much emphasis on one person. "I think the public wants stars," he said, "[but] it's not a good thing. We should be celebrating how wonderful the orchestra is ... Ultimately what's going to endure, long past Delfs, is the SPCO and the community. What we hope is no matter who's on the podium, people will come because it's the SPCO." With the growing realization that Delfs was not working out, Coppock began making plans to institute some of the more radical changes he had set aside earlier in his tenure.

Coppock had begun laying the groundwork for change during his first weeks on the job. Inspired by the opportunity to win a major grant from the Andrew W. Mellon Foundation (Mellon had recently launched a new program aimed at strengthening the artistic identities of American orchestras), Coppock and his staff embarked on a long and sometimes painful process of institutional self-evaluation. By early 2000, he had come to the conclusion that the SPCO must reject its previous "star-based" leadership philosophy and shift its artistic focus to "the ensemble itself."' As he saw it, the orchestra had no choice but to move away from traditional "hierarchical artistic and executive leadership models" and put more artistic "power" in the hands of the musicians.

Coppock's reluctance to act precipitously had led him to table such radical ideas and to opt instead for what he later called the "utterly traditional" hiring of Andreas Delfs. Delfs had accepted the job knowing that the orchestra intended to involve its musicians more fully in artistic decision-making, but he was also fully aware that he retained most of the powers and responsibilities traditionally assigned to an orchestral music director.

He was in charge. Now, at the end of Delfs's first season, tradition was on the way out.

In the summer of 2002, negotiations got underway on a new contract for the SPCO's musicians. In the months that followed, the players and management engaged in a series of unusually harmonious discussions led by an industrial psychologist. Although the negotiations covered basic issues such as compensation and health care, much of the focus was on artistic leadership. By the end of January 2003, both sides agreed the musicians would assume the bulk of the orchestra's artistic decision-making power. In the final contract, completed three months later, the musicians agreed to accept an 18 percent pay cut. (An economic downturn exacerbated by the September 11 attacks had left the orchestra with its first deficit in ten years.) Herb Winslow, the musicians' lead negotiator, supported the agreement but acknowledged that some players were skeptical of the new balance of power. "Some look on it as a scary proposition," he said. "It's one of those things where you know it's going to be an adventure. You just don't know how it's going to turn out."

The new contract, with its power-shifting arrangement, left Andreas Delfs in an uncomfortable state of limbo. Coppock publicly insisted that the agreement would "not diminish Andreas's influence on programming," but his statements to the press concealed what was going on behind the scenes: He and Delfs already had mutually agreed to end Delfs's directorship. What remained unclear was when Delfs would leave and who—if anyone—would replace him.

Delfs had two years remaining on his contract and was in a position to make life difficult for the orchestra if he chose to do so. Instead, he agreed to assist Coppock in making the SPCO's transition to a new artistic leadership scheme as smooth as possible. "It could have been a really unpleasant parting of the ways," Coppock said, "but it turned out be a perfectly fine parting of the ways because Delfs said: 'This isn't right. You need some other structure.'"

Coppock had long been intrigued by Deborah Borda's decision to create the artistic commission, or triumvirate, in the late 1980s, but he knew the experiment had lasted only a few years and was widely deemed a failure. Still, he was convinced that Borda was onto something—that a chamber orchestra could not achieve its full potential under the baton of a single, all-powerful music director. As the months went by, a consensus began to develop among the musicians and management that the orchestra needed not one, but multiple artistic leaders. The biggest pushback came from board members, many of whom wondered whether the orchestra could succeed without a music director to serve as its public face. Coppock argued that traditional music directorships often disrupted ties with community, since the switch from one conductor to another almost always resulted in a drastic shift in artistic direction. Beside that, he added, an orchestra that hitched its identity too closely to a single conductor risked losing its identity altogether. He pointed to former creative chair Bobby McFerrin's farewell concert in 2001 as a case in point.

Now Bobby McFerrin—enormously gifted guy—was not even the music director, and yet he had become in some ways the public relations symbol of the orchestra. And when he did his farewell concert at Orchestra Hall, there was a huge photograph of him above the fold on the front page of the newspaper. That was a public relations nightmare for the SPCO because what it said was, the SPCO has just lost its leader. And he wasn't even the leader. Thinking strategically, I said, "That's a disaster."

In the end, Coppock won over the skeptics on the board. The musicians agreed—with no small amount of trepidation—to scrap the position of music director and assume greater artistic control. The SPCO was poised to head off in a direction that no American orchestra had ever gone.

After several years of cautious consideration, The Saint Paul Chamber Orchestra plunged ahead with its new plan for the future. At a news conference in early January 2004, the orchestra announced it was dissolving the position of music director and replacing it with a group of five renowned "artistic partners"—violinist Joshua Bell, oboist Douglas Boyd, composer-pianist Stephen Prutsman, conductor Roberto Abbado, and conductor Nicholas McGegan (the director of the SPCO's Baroque Series). Most of the administrative decisions previously made by the music director would now be split between two committees—each comprising three musicians and two management representatives. The artistic vision committee would be responsible for programming, touring, and recording. The artistic personnel committee would take charge of auditions, tenure, and other musical personnel matters.

The SPCO's new artistic partners plan was designed, in part, to give the musicians a greater voice in the orchestra's artistic direction. Shown here are Nina Tso-Ning Fan, and Thomas Kornacker, violins (above), and Principal Second Violin Dale Barltrop (below).

The orchestra presented a strikingly united front as it unveiled its plans. Joining Bruce Coppock for the announcement of what he called a "marriage of polygamy" were board chairman Lowell Noteboom, violinist Thomas Kornacker, and—to the surprise of many—Andreas Delfs. Under the new leadership scheme, Delfs would continue in an informal consulting role with the SPCO, but his tenure as music director would come to an abrupt end. The orchestra was essentially buying out the final year of his contract. Not that he seemed to mind. "I was very happy to encourage them and be a catalyst," he said. "This new model is certainly not for every institution, but for the SPCO, it's not only inevitable, it's long overdue. I admire them for their courage and their guts, and I will watch with excitement and help any way I can."

The clear message was that now, it was all about the musicians.

"The musicians here are now totally involved, probably more involved than in any other orchestra in the country," Noteboom said.

"The musicians now control their destiny," Kornacker added.

Coppock concurred: "If musicians have a say about who they collaborate and perform with," he said, "we think it'll lead to better concerts and a more stable face for the orchestra."

With all the hoopla surrounding the announcement of the new artistic partners arrangement, another radical transformation—this one of the SPCO board of directors—went largely unnoticed by the public. Under Noteboom's leadership, the board had decided to reject much of the conventional wisdom regarding orchestra governance and remake itself as a more dynamic force. It eliminated term limits, extending the tenure of the board chairman beyond the traditional two years. (Noteboom eventually served more than six years.) It set new and rigorous expectations for all board members. ("We ask our board to say 'yes' three times," Coppock explained. "Yes to giving until it hurts, yes to participating in a *lot* of meetings, and yes to doing the work.") It also transferred effective decision-making authority from the executive committee to the full board. Coppock was thrilled with the results. "No executive director alone can turn an organization around, let alone take it to the next level," he said. "To be effective at either task, an executive director requires strong, engaged board leadership that will test his or her thinking, challenge, mentor and help him or her grow." With the board's transformation complete, he said he had "blessedly been the beneficiary of all those things."

Living Up to the Image

The decision to eliminate the music director position and replace it with a group of artistic partners constituted a momentous break with the past, but it was just one of several significant choices that transformed the SPCO during its fifth decade. In nearly every case, the changes resulted from a desire to maximize the characteristics that made the orchestra distinctive.

Almost from the moment it was conceived, the SPCO had thought of itself as unique—as a band of musicians, poles apart from what was perceived to be its main competitor, the Minnesota Orchestra. The pursuit of the Mellon grant during the early 2000s had forced the orchestra to ask some tough questions about itself, and that process of self-evaluation had convinced Bruce Coppock and others that for most of its history the SPCO had often failed to live up to its own image. "There was this disconnect between the behavior and structure and artistic output of the organization, and what it said about its own distinctiveness," Coppock said. "A big disconnect." The self-evaluation process prompted the board, under the leadership of Chairman John Huss, to launch a new strategic plan.

Using a metaphor that would be repeated countless times in the years to come, the task force that drew up the plan asserted that the SPCO should "make itself as

distinctive from the Minnesota Orchestra as the Walker Art
Center is from the Minneapolis Institute of Arts." In other
words, the task force said, the SPCO should make sure that
it acted like a chamber orchestra, not a symphony orchestra.
That meant, among other things, that it should play in
venues that showed off its music-making to best advantage.

For years, the SPCO had made regular appearances at
Minneapolis's Orchestra Hall, despite a nearly unanimous
opinion that Orchestra Hall was far too big for a chamber
orchestra. The task force concluded that the SPCO's
concerts there invited "inappropriate comparisons [that]
do not serve the goal of differentiating the SPCO's
artistic profile from that of the Minnesota Orchestra." As
the strategic plan suggested, the SPCO eliminated its
Orchestra Hall series in 2002 and replaced it with a new

The SPCO introduced a new Sunday
performance series at the University of
Minnesota's Ted Mann Concert Hall during
the 2002-2003 season.

series at the Ted Mann Concert Hall on the University of Minnesota campus. With its
superior acoustics and a seating capacity of 1,200, Ted Mann was, in the words of the
strategic plan, "a nearly ideal space for the SPCO"—at least in Minneapolis. Saint Paul
was another matter.

Although the Ordway Center for the Performing Arts was, in many respects, the
SPCO's Saint Paul home, it had never fit the orchestra as well as many had hoped. It
was a beautiful but acoustically flawed multi-purpose facility, forced to serve both as a
musical concert hall and a theatrical space. (Coppock said the situation at the Ordway
was "a little like putting a golf match, a football game, and a basketball game in the same
stadium.") Its seating capacity of 1,900 made it too big to create the kind of intimate
atmosphere small orchestras like the SPCO preferred.

Driven by its new determination to play in venues that highlighted its
distinctiveness, the SPCO arranged to extend the Ordway stage twenty-one feet into
the audience and trim the hall's seating capacity to about 1,400. The reconfiguration
succeeded in creating a more intimate concert-going experience and improved the
acoustics, especially on the floor level, where, in the words of the *Saint Paul Pioneer Press,*
"patrons are finally hearing the vibrant sounds they paid for."

Even with the addition of the thrust stage, the Ordway remained ill suited for
concerts featuring smaller ensembles and chamber repertoire. Its dependence on multiple
users, including traveling Broadway productions, also made scheduling rehearsal time
difficult. (The SPCO and the Ordway would continue to clash over scheduling conflicts
until 2007 when they—along with the Minnesota Opera and the Schubert Club—
formed a non-profit partnership to sort out their differences.) The orchestra needed a
home of its own—one it didn't have to share with other arts organizations.

In 2004, its wishes finally came true with the construction of a new 250-seat
rehearsal and concert space in the Hamm Building, where the SPCO kept its
administrative offices. The SPCO Center, as the new venue was known, made use of

The Huss Music Room in the SPCO Center.

Above: Lowell Noteboom, John Huss, Ruth Huss, and Bruce Coppock at the dedication of the Huss Music Room in the new SPCO Center, 2005. Over the previous two decades, the Husses' leadership giving had helped stabilize the orchestra's finances and provided the foundation for its artistic maturation. In the words of SPCO Vice President and Chief Operating Officer Jon Limbacher, "We wouldn't be where we are without them."

two floors that had been left empty since the demolition of the Hamm Building's longtime centerpiece—the Paramount movie theater (originally known as the Capitol)—in 1965. Its Huss Music Room (named for former board chairman John Huss and his wife, Ruth, in recognition of their lifetime support of the SPCO) featured exposed beams and air ducts, wooden acoustic panels, and a thirty-two-foot ceiling. It gave the musicians their first dedicated rehearsal space and provided a nearly perfect setting for the orchestra's Chamber Music Series. The *Saint Paul Pioneer Press's* Rob Hubbard reported that the SPCO Center boasted "an immediacy the spacious and formal-feeling Ordway can't match," and that it was inspiring "many a longtime SPCO subscriber to shift downtown destinations on their concert-going calendars."

The SPCO now had its own dedicated rehearsal and performance space. It had found a way to make the Ordway more artistically hospitable and abandoned Orchestra Hall in favor of the Ted Mann Concert Hall. There was just one more question to answer regarding the orchestra's performance venues: What about the neighborhoods?

Ever since the days of Leopold Sipe, Dennis Russell Davies, and Music on the Move, the SPCO had made a point of taking music out of the concert hall and into the community. Over the years, the orchestra's commitment to community music making had waxed and waned. During much of the 1980s and 1990s, the orchestra seemed to send the subliminal message that concerts played at neighborhood venues were not as important as those played at the Ordway. Neighborhood performance spaces such as Temple Israel in Minneapolis, Saint Paul's United Church of Christ in Saint Paul, and Wooddale Church in Eden Prairie were relegated to hosting mostly lightly attended concerts—especially Baroque Series performances—that lacked the much wider appeal of Ordway concerts.

The 2002 strategic plan touched only briefly on the role that neighborhood venues should play in the orchestra's future. Soon after the plan's release, a separate task force weighed in on the issue, and its conclusion was unequivocal. "We realize being rooted in the neighborhoods and suburbs is part and parcel of the special connection SPCO has with the community," Coppock told the *St. Paul Pioneer Press*. "It's one of our core values. It's so engrained and embedded in who we are, we don't even think about whether it's the right thing to do."

After years of downplaying its neighborhood venues, the SPCO suddenly began adding new ones. Trinity Lutheran Church in Stillwater was the first. Then Wayzata Community Church in Wayzata, Shepherd of the Valley Lutheran Church in Apple Valley, Bigelow Chapel in New Brighton, and Benson Great Hall at Bethel University in Arden Hills. Under the orchestra's new approach, the neighborhood venues began hosting concerts as stimulating and diverse in their programming as any presented at the Ordway. Adding to their appeal was a new policy slashing ticket prices at the suburban venues by as much as 45 percent. Suburban audiences seemed to appreciate the convenience of having great, affordably priced music come to them.

"It's nice to have a bit of this kind of culture in our neck of the woods," said a concertgoer from Apple Valley.

"Having the SPCO here has created moments for people in the community to share something they love doing and stay close to home," observed another fan from Stillwater.

Even the musicians got caught up in the neighborhood mood. Bassist Fred Bretschger, for one, was delighted to discover how enthusiastic the suburban audiences could be. "They were clapping between every movement, [but] that doesn't bother me," he said following a performance of Mozart's Symphony No. 36 in C Major ("Linz") in Apple Valley. "Some people say, 'Oh, you should wait till the end of the whole piece,' but I figure they were liking it."

The new commitment to neighborhood venues, with emphasis on low prices and vibrant programming, was part of a broad effort to remove what Bruce Coppock and others called the "barriers" between the orchestra and its audience. It wasn't just in the suburbs where the barriers were coming down. In 2005, for example, the orchestra introduced a new concept, "Jazzed-Up Fridays," to its Ordway series. On certain weekends, concertgoers were given two options after intermission: They could either return to their seats for the second half of the program or remain in the lobby to listen to live jazz. Not everyone was enamored with the idea (three years earlier Coppock himself had publicly fretted that, in the race to create more casual settings, orchestras were sending the message that "the music isn't enough"), but the results at the box office were hard to deny. In the five years after the orchestra began making changes spelled out in the 2002 strategic plan, its subscriber base grew by nearly 40 percent. The hope was that many of the new subscribers would eventually become sustaining contributors. "Any cultural institution, is ultimately dependent on a very high percentage of the consumers paying twice," Coppock explained. "Once for the ticket and once for the contribution."

Longtime board member, Dr. Art Kaemmer, and his wife Martha Kaemmer pose with Principal Oboist Kathryn Greenbank at the SPCO's 2006 Opening Night dinner. The Hulings, Rice, and Kaemmer families have been significant and dedicated supporters over most of the SPCO's history.

Making It Work

Although the SPCO's audiences seemed to take the switch to the new artistic partners scheme in stride, the musicians needed time to acclimate themselves to the new reality. After years of subjugating themselves to the whims of various music directors, they suddenly had the power—through the artistic vision committee and the artistic personnel committee—to influence crucial decisions affecting their future and the future of the orchestra. Horn player Herb Winslow said the main challenge facing the musicians was "learning to disagree." Violinist Leslie Shank worried that musicians were "being put into roles they weren't hired for." Shank's colleague Thomas Kornacker acknowledged that some of musicians remained skeptical about the new system—especially the artistic personnel committee with its hiring and firing power—but he insisted the change was paying off.

> *It's working. On a scale of ten, I'd give it an eight. I mean, we came from nothing in terms of responsibility. The artistic personnel committee had to tackle instituting a new audition process, a new tenure process. They're now working on something we call a feedback process that will allow the musicians to interact with each other on what I think will be a much higher level of artistic planning. They have enormous challenges in front of them, which we gave them and assumed that it would take time for them to work out. For instance, they spent three or four meetings on the chamber music question— plans to put more chamber music into the programs—where it would have been hoped that just one meeting would get it fleshed out.*

Even as the musicians grappled with their new responsibilities, they began forging relationships with their new artistic partners that were unlike any they had with their former music directors. The fact that they had a voice in the selection of each partner gave them extra incentive to make the relationships work. They also enjoyed the artistic variety that came with multiple conductors. "They can each do what they like," bassoonist Chuck Ullery said of the artistic partners. "If Josh Bell wants to do standard rep and Nic McGegan just Baroque, that's fine."

Artistic Partner Nicholas McGegan conducts the SPCO during a concert at Temple Israel, 2003.

Likewise, the partners seemed to thrive in a system that granted them wide artistic freedom without saddling them with the administrative responsibilities of a traditional music director. "We're here at the specific invitation of the orchestra, so you get away from the sense of employer and employee," Douglas Boyd explained. "Also, the variety is more stimulating. I feel like the musicians are delighted to see me, rather than, 'Oh, my God, not another week with him!'"

Still, the new leadership format, with its emphasis on collaboration, took some getting used to. Rehearsals—especially those in which the artistic partner chose not to conduct from a podium—posed some of the biggest challenges.

No podium necessary. Artistic Partner
Joshua Bell with the SPCO, 2005.

"[They] can be a little more chaotic," Concertmaster Steven Copes admitted. "It takes more time, but it gets everyone more involved than when there's just one conductor saying, 'This is how it goes.'"

The results come performance time seemed to justify the SPCO's embrace of the artistic partnership concept. The orchestra opened its 2004-2005 season, its first under the new leadership structure, with Douglas Boyd on the podium and soloist Pierre-Laurent Aimard on the piano. It was an evening of Mozart, the overture from *The Magic Flute* and his Piano Concerto No. 27, and Schubert, Symphony No. 9, (the "Great"), and Twin Cities critics were impressed. "Boyd has obviously established a quick rapport with these musicians, who played with spirit and precision all evening," the *Star Tribune's* Michael Anthony wrote. "Boyd himself made a lively presence at the podium: energetic, confident and full of ideas about the music at hand." As the months went by, local critics, including Rob Hubbard of the *St. Paul Pioneer Press,* chronicled the debut of each successive artistic partner.

Nicholas McGegan, displaying his passion for Baroque, punched up a Handel concerto to the point where he was "swaying with elbows and knees bent like a sailor yo-hoing his way through a chantey."

Stephen Prutsman

Roberto Abbado

Joshua Bell led the orchestra "in one of the most exhilarating interpretations of Beethoven's Seventh Symphony you may ever have the fortune to experience."

Stephen Prutsman displayed "both the tremendous technical skill of a classical virtuoso and the explosive abandon of a jazz giant" in a memorable jazz band version of George Gershwin's *Rhapsody in Blue.*

Roberto Abbado opened a four-week Mozart festival with "the air of authority one associates with the great maestros," cutting "a magnetic figure on the podium for orchestra and audience alike."

All in all, Hubbard wrote, the SPCO's artistic partnership experiment looked to be a success—one that forced concertgoers to "rethink whether following the vision of one leader is appropriate for this small, eclectic ensemble."

It wasn't just Twin Cities concertgoers who were enjoying the fruits of the SPCO's artistic experiment. For nearly a decade, the orchestra had touted itself in public and private as "America's Chamber Orchestra." At first, the claim seemed little more than a slogan to rally the troops; now it was taking on real meaning. For the first time in years, the SPCO was making its presence known both nationally and internationally. It established a multi-year residency program at the University of Chicago in which it served as a laboratory orchestra for doctoral candidates in composition. In 2007, it made its first European tour in nine years. A year later, it returned to New York after a similarly long hiatus. In his review of the orchestra's appearance at Zankel Hall, the *New Yorker's* Russell Platt wrote: "It's safe to say that America's only full-time chamber orchestra … which hadn't played in New York in a decade—is back on the block in a serious way."

Continuo

It was one of the last weekends of the 2006-2007 season, and Bruce Coppock and the rest of the SPCO management team were nervous about how it would go. Joshua Bell was wrapping up his three-year run as artistic partner, and his farewell performances posed a potential public relations hazard. Although the orchestra had insisted all along that its new artistic leadership format represented a rejection of the old "star" system, with its reliance on big-name conductors and soloists, Bell was by almost any definition of the word a star. There was a danger that the news media and the audience would treat his departure as the end of an era, much as they had when Bobby McFerrin left in 2001. "We were worried about loss of audience," Coppock said.

The Friday evening performance began with Mozart's Symphony No. 38 in D ("Prague"). As he had on numerous occasions since his debut as artistic partner, Bell led the orchestra from the concertmaster's chair—a first among equals. "It was fun to watch Bell play sitting down," *Mpls St. Paul* magazine columnist Lani Willis wrote. "It looked hard for him. Maybe a little restrictive. All his energy seemed to want to rise."

For the next piece, Max Bruch's Violin Concerto No. 1 in G Minor, Bell was on his feet, front and center. When he wasn't soloing, he was leading the orchestra with his

Douglas Boyd, shown here during a concert in early 2009, was one of the SPCO's five original artistic partners. The others were Joshua Bell, Stephen Prutsman, Roberto Abbado, and Nicholas McGegan.

bow, his eyes, and his body. There was no baton to be seen. "You can see the beauty of the music all over his face—its romance and its anguish," Willis wrote. "Oh, and what you hear! The long, legato lines of the Adagio movement seemed to stretch on forever, and the audience held its breath." When it was over, the audience seemed to jump to its feet. Bell turned to the packed house and beamed. And then he was gone.

Bell knew when to step aside. His absence during the second half of the program served as an unmistakable reminder that the orchestra would go on without him. As Steven Copes, Sabina Thatcher, and Ronald Thomas played Beethoven in the main hall and Chris Brown and his band played jazz in the upper foyer (it was a Jazzed Up Friday), Bell sat at a table downstairs, signing copies of his latest CD for a small group of fans. Fears that his departure would overshadow the orchestra had proved unfounded. "It was a non-event," Coppock said.

The artistic partnership system was helping the orchestra maintain artistic continuity, just as Coppock had hoped it would. Joshua Bell was leaving, but a new artistic partner, soprano Dawn Upshaw, had already signed on to take his place. Over time, the roster of artistic partners would continue to evolve with the additions of Pierre-Laurent Aimard, pianist Christian Zacharias, and former Minnesota Orchestra music director Edo de Waart.

It appeared that the SPCO had strengthened its commitment to artistic continuity in other ways as well. Over the years, the orchestra had gone through managing directors

Pierre-Laurent Aimard joined the SPCO as an artistic partner in 2007.

Soprano Dawn Upshaw was the first female member of the SPCO's artistic partner team.

at a dizzying pace. Stephen Sell had lasted only four years; Deborah Borda, less than three; Brent Assink, a little more than five. Bruce Coppock understood the benefits of longevity. He knew that without a music director overseeing all things artistic, the SPCO needed an administrator who could set long-term artistic goals and put the orchestra in position to achieve them. "You can only make sustained progress," he said, "if the executive director really owns the responsibility of the long term musical and artistic health of the organization." In 2006, Coppock signed a new contract that would keep him with the SPCO through the 2011-2012 season. The orchestra's revolving managerial door had officially stopped spinning.

On the eve of its fiftieth anniversary season, The Saint Paul Chamber Orchestra had ample justification to look back with pride at what it had accomplished over the previous five decades. In some ways, little had changed since that first concert in 1959, when the program notes declared with proper Minnesotan modesty that the SPCO would devote itself to "the wonderful literature, both classic and contemporary, that is not ordinarily played by large symphonies." Over the years, the orchestra had set its sights considerably higher. Earlier in the decade, members of the strategic planning committee had sharply disagreed about the wording of one of the plan's main strategic goals. Should the SPCO be "*a* symbol of cultural excellence in the Twin Cities" or "*the* symbol of cultural excellence in the Twin Cities"? In the end, the "the's" prevailed by a vote of seven to six. As Bruce Coppock was fond of saying, the SPCO needed to "stand for something."

Coppock fully expected to stay with the SPCO through the end of his contract in 2012, to make sure the orchestra continued to pursue the audacious goals it had set for itself, but life intervened. At the final board meeting of the 2007-2008 season, he announced he was stepping down. Recent tests had determined that a previously diagnosed cancer had metastasized. He was leaving "to devote all of my energies to my family." In a press release announcing his retirement, Coppock expressed his conviction that the orchestra had made "very real strides in creating an artistically vibrant, financially robust cultural institution which will serve the Twin Cities and international music communities for the next 50 years."

The musicians, staff, and board members of the SPCO had every reason to believe that the orchestra—under its new president and managing director, former Minnesota Public Radio executive Sarah Lutman—would continue to navigate the course that Coppock been instrumental in establishing. The budget was balanced. Subscriptions were up. By most accounts, the level of musicianship had never been higher. There were even plans in the works to expand the Ordway's 306-seat McKnight Theatre into a thousand-seat concert hall that would serve as the SPCO's primary performance space. The expansion plan grew out of an unprecedented 2007 agreement, facilitated by a group of St. Paul civic leaders, to repair the Ordway's deteriorating relationships with its primary tenants—the Schubert Club, the Minnesota Opera, and the SPCO. Coppock called the agreement and the non-profit partnership it created a true "civic success story."

After enduring five decades marked by heady successes and nearly catastrophic failures, the orchestra had found a way to balance artistic risk-taking with institutional stability.

In February 2006, the orchestra had received a letter from a pair of concertgoers, Doug Wallace and Peggy Hunter. Wallace and Hunter had attended a concert featuring solo turns by the SPCO's Ruggero Allifranchini, Ronald Thomas, Steven Copes, and Dale Barltrop, and the experience had inspired them to write.

> *Dear Musicians,*
> *Especially during the last two years, we've been inspired by your imaginative programming and spectacular performances. It is obvious that this orchestra is something special and world-class in the way it interprets composers and conveys the moods and colors of the compositions. And it just keeps getting better and better.*
>
> *But last Saturday night, you soared into the stratosphere. The prodigious energy and stream of talent of the ensemble not only inspired the audience— it took us into a sublime place that for many will be one of those electrifying moments that will never be forgotten.*

After heaping praise on the ensemble's performance of Astor Piazzolla's *Four Seasons of Buenos Aires,* Wallace and Hunter closed with a coda worth remembering.

"If the SPCO can keep [its] collective gifts together—indeed it doesn't need guest soloists with the talent in the orchestra—we are in for many more of these wonderful moments of grace," they wrote. "We can't wait."

Bruce Coppock
President and Managing Director, 1999-2008

———

Bruce Coppock claimed upon his hiring as the The Saint Paul Chamber Orchestra's new president and managing director in 1999 that he had been a fan of the orchestra since the early 1970s, during the first years of Dennis Russell Davies's tenure. Coppock was, at the time, a student cellist at the New England Conservatory of Music and he appreciated Davies's adventurous spirit. After arriving in Saint Paul, he frequently referred to the Davies years as the "heyday" of the orchestra.

Still, Coppock never believed that the SPCO could get where it needed to go by simply installing another adventurous, Davies-style music director. With his background as a professional musician (his playing career ended abruptly in 1990 when he injured his left hand in a car accident), Coppock was convinced that the orchestra would reach its full potential only if it broke free of standard orchestral operating procedures.

It had always struck me about orchestras, both from the time I played in the Boston Symphony to the time I managed in Saint Louis, that having other people make decisions about what you're doing all the time is a stultifying experience. Even if those decisions are made well, even if those decisions are implemented by inspiring people, at the end of the day, as an orchestra player, you are a non-participant in those decisions.

Coppock believed that the new artistic partners plan put in place in 2004 would free the SPCO's musicians from excessive top-down decision-making and "unleash their creativity." At the same time, he realized that someone had to assume many of the artistic and administrative leadership duties traditionally performed by the music director, and he was more than willing to do so. "Someone needs to herd all those calves," he explained. "Someone needs to provide some cohesiveness. Someone needs to say, 'Yes, but. Nice idea, but it doesn't quite work.'"

By the time Coppock stepped down in 2008, he had established himself as an uncommonly creative and effective administrator—not just in the Twin Cities, but throughout the country. "There is no one else like him in the field of American orchestras today," said Lowell Noteboom, who became chair of the League of American Orchestras after stepping down as SPCO board chair in 2007. "He is widely admired and consulted by his counterparts across the country. He is one of the most creative and insightful leaders in our industry. Bruce has not only totally reshaped the SPCO, but he has made the SPCO the role model for the industry."

Review

Tsontakis: Violin Concerto No. 2; The Saint Paul Chamber Orchestra, Douglas Boyd conducting.

Composer George Tsontakis possesses a singular ability to integrate themes,

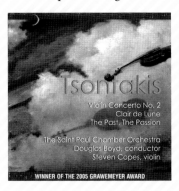

fragments, techniques, and aesthetics from across the history of Western art music, dabble in the jazz idiom, and tip his hat to some modern techniques. Though many composers have used models from the past to influence and drive their own compositions, Tsontakis does all of this without it ever seeming as if to rely exclusively on the past or make references so heavy-handed that listeners think that he is incapable of original thought. Quite the contrary; Tsontaskis's works and musical style are completely his own. Although highly chromatic, rhythmically and contrapuntally complex, his compositions are generally quite accessible and usually quite emotionally evocative. This album of his award-winning works is no exception. Performed by The Saint Paul Chamber Orchestra, by whom the Second Violin Concerto and "Clair de Lune" were commissioned, this album is an exceptional introduction to Tsontakis for anyone who has not already had the pleasure. The Violin Concerto, performed by the orchestra's concert master Steven Copes, earned Tsontakis the Grawemeyer Award. Although entitled a concerto, this highly expressive piece is truly more of a rhapsodic dialogue between the solo violin and orchestra rather than a showpiece for the violin. Throughout the album, the SPCO proves their affinity for the composer via highly committed, detailed performances that go well beyond simply playing the notes, instead drawing listeners in and telling a story through Tsontakis's music.

—*All Music Guide,* 2007

Contributors

———

We gratefully acknowledge the following contributors to The Saint Paul Chamber Orchestra's 50th Anniversary season and all of the celebratory activities taking place during this landmark year.

Fred C. and Katherine B. Andersen Foundation
Amphion Foundation
Martha and Bruce Atwater
Gordon and Jo Bailey
Thomas M. and Barbara Brown
City of Saint Paul Cultural STAR Program
Lynn and Sandra Davis*
Julia W. Dayton*
Delta Air Lines
Joan R. Duddingston
Alfred and Ingrid Lenz Harrison*
James and Kathryn Haymaker*
Anna M. Heilmaier Charitable Foundation, U.S. Bank N.A., Trustee
Amy Hubbard*
Ruth and John Huss*
The Art and Martha Kaemmer Fund of HRK Foundation*
Erwin and Miriam Kelen*
John and Karen R. Larsen
Richard Coyle Lilly Foundation
Leland T. Lynch and Terry Saario Fund of The Minneapolis Foundation*
Stephen H. and Kathi Austin Mahle
The Andrew W. Mellon Foundation
Alfred P. and Ann M. Moore
Lowell and Sonja Noteboom
RBC Wealth Management
Mary E. Schaffner and Robert L. Lee
Fred and Gloria Sewell
Travelers
Joanne and Philip Von Blon
Jane and Dobson West*
The Charles A. Weyerhaeuser Memorial Foundation

* Gift made in honor of Bruce H. Coppock's tenure as President and Managing Director

Photo Credits

———

The Saint Paul Chamber Orchestra
4-5, 8-9, 20, 21, 27, 29 (both), 31, 33, 34 (both), 35, 37, 39, 40, 42, 44, 47, 48, 49, 51, 52, 56, 58, 62, 64, 66, 67, 69. 70 (both), 71, 73, 74, 75, 79, 80, 84, 86, 90 (below), 91, 94 (below), 97 (above), 100, 118 (above)

For The Saint Paul Chamber Orchestra
    Felix Broede, 119 (below)
    Donald Dietz, 87
    Jeffrey Grosscup, 90 (above)
    Greg Helgeson, 97 (below), 101 (below)
    Bruce Kluckhohn, 108
    Ann Marsden, 120, 122
    John Palumbo, 94 (above), 95
    Rat Race Studios, 119 (above)
    Sara Rubinstein, 111 (both), 117, 118 (below), 124-125
    Tim Rummelhoff, 98 (both), 99
    Rich Ryan, 104, 113, 116
    Eric Saulitis, 102
    Keith Saunders, 82, 88, 96, 101 (above)
    Stan Waldhauser, 106, 114 (both), 115

Minnesota Historical Society, *Pioneer Press* photo collection
22, 23, 36, 43, 45, 63

Minnesota Historical Society, *Star Tribune* photo collection
26, 55, 60, 78

Note to researchers: A complete manuscript of this book, including citations, is available in the collections of the Minnesota Historical Society.